THE CLICK OF THE STICK

THE CLICK OF THE STICK

Walking the Welsh coastline from
Chester to Chepstow.

GRAHAM BELL

authorHOUSE®

AuthorHouse™
1663 Liberty Drive
Bloomington, IN 47403
www.authorhouse.com
Phone: 1-800-839-8640

First published by AuthorHouse 10/04/2011

ISBN: 978-1-4567-8819-3 (sc)

Printed in the United States of America

Any people depicted in stock imagery provided by Thinkstock are models, and such images are being used for illustrative purposes only.
Certain stock imagery © Thinkstock.

This book is printed on acid-free paper.

This book is dedicated to the memory of a
wonderful friend - David Pridmore (1936 - 2005)

THE BOOK, THE AUTHOR'S FIRST, TELLS OF THE
ADVENTURES OF A COUPLE OF AGEING EX RAF PALS
AS THEY EMBARKED ON A SPECIAL JOURNEY—FOR THEM
THAT IS.

THEY DECIDED TO WALK THE ENTIRE WELSH COASTLINE
FROM THE DEE ESTUARY IN THE NORTH TO CHEPSTOW
IN THE SOUTH. A FURTHER BOOK TELLS OF WALKING
THE SOUTH WEST COASTAL PATH FROM MINEHEAD TO
POOLE.

THE TOTAL JOURNEY OF SOME 1500 MILES WOULD TAKE
THEM NOT ONLY INTO ALL THE WELL KNOWN MAJOR
HOLIDAY RESORTS, BUT OFTEN INTO AREAS THEY HAD
NEVER EVEN HEARD OF.

THERE WOULD BE A VARIETY OF CHARACTERS TO MEET
AND ODD PLACES OF ACCOMMODATION AT WHICH TO
STAY BUT, ABOVE ALL, STUNNING SCENERY COULD
BE EXPECTED AS THESE UNPROVEN LONG DISTANCE
WALKERS PLODDED ONWARDS.

THEIR MAIN INTENTION WAS TO ENJOY IT AND HAVE
PLENTY OF LAUGHS ON THE WAY.

Graham Bell was born in 1936 in the Potteries. He was educated at a local Grammar School and afterwards he embarked on a long career in the Pottery Industry. On reaching his 18th birthday he was conscripted into the RAF for 2 years, where he was to meet the man who was to be his good friend and colleague for the next 40 years—David Pridmore—the man who was destined to be his walking companion.

Graham still lives in the Potteries with his wife Jean, whom he married in 1959. They have 3 daughters, 3 grand-daughters and 2 grandsons, who all live nearby. At present his hobbies include, as well as walking, water colour painting; gardening; Crown Green bowling, and who knows in the future, more writing!

INTRODUCTION

It all started early in 1989.

One day my old RAF mate, David Pridmore, rang and out of the blue asked if I fancied doing a walk with him—a long distance walk. He sounded serious about it and, after the initial shock, I warmed to the idea.

As owners of well-loved dogs who needed plenty of exercise, both of us had walked hundreds of miles over the years, albeit perhaps only 3 or 4 miles a day. Walking was, we found, a most enjoyable experience, a way to see the countryside, so a long distance walk seemed a good idea, a special project if you like. By Summer, we started to get serious and do something about it.

But what walk could we do?. It needed to be thought out really well, particularly as Dave lived in Loughborough and I in Stoke. My wife, Jean and I went over to Dave and Norma's for a few days and, with the help of maps and books about walking, borrowed from the library, a plan began to take shape.

Most distance walkers choose the well trodden paths—The Pennine Way, Offa's Dyke, The Ridgeway, Pembrokeshire Coast Path and many more.

Graham Bell

So what walk could we do that was a bit different?

Both of us had always loved the sea and it's relaxing nature, so coast was preferred to inland. But which coast.

Obviously, easy access in a reasonable amount of travelling time was very important. The solution was clear—Wales. Which part of it?—all of it. We would walk the whole coastline of Wales.

Looking at a general map of Wales, we could see that not all areas have a natural coastal walk, that is we couldn't expect to have clifftop or beach walking for the whole 750 odd miles, and so we would have to devise the route ourselves, the object being to walk as close as allowed to the coastline. Ordnance Survey Pathfinder maps would be our guide.

Then there were other things to take into consideration. How long would it take us? How would we get to lodgings etc?

We felt we could manage to get away three or four weekends a year. Our aim was to try and finish it in six years, doing about 120 miles a year—about 30 to 35 miles in a weekend.

With regard to accommodation and how to reach it, this meant getting hold of brochures for various areas and also local bus timetables. Basically the idea was to park the car, bus it out to a start point some 15 to 20 miles away. then walk back to the car and drive to a pre-booked B&B.

We decided our venture could be done theoretically, but practically—well, only time would tell.

The route pencilled in as being the most accessibly viable coastline would take us from Saughall on the Dee estuary, west of Chester, to Chepstow, and we would also include the Isle of Anglesey. Due to travelling, timing and locations, we decided we would not necessarily follow the coastline in sequence.

The decision to 'go for it' was made, and October 7th would be departure day, and Benllech on Anglesey was determined as our starting point. We decided on Anglesey which has approximately a 120 mile coastline, because we felt that if we couldn't or didn't want to continue the venture, we would have had a little fun and lost nothing.

What follows then, is an account of what happened on our journey through Wales.

CHAPTER ONE

October 1989

Day 1 Benllech to Menai Bridge 18 miles

The next few weeks or quite exciting as we made meticulous plans and there were several phone calls between Dave and I to iron out as many details as possible. After all, we'd never done anything like this before and we wanted, as far as we could, to get it right.

We'd bought the necessary maps of the area, a route had been worked out and the accommodation booked. All that remained was to get out and do it.

Departure of day had arrived.

We couldn't have chosen worse weather as we started out from Stoke at about 5.30 am on a cold, dark morning driving into heavy rain and mist plus strong winds. Were we mad or not, we thought, but we were not chickening out now.

Our intention was to drive to our B&B accommodation at Benllech, catch the 8.05 am bus to Menai Bridge and then walk back to Benllech. All would have gone to plan except for our first mistake. We decided to leave the A55 and have a our breakfast on the seafront at Rhos-on-sea. There weren't

many people about, just at the local milk float
and a couple of dog walkers, as we sat enjoying
our bacon sandwiches. The rain had actually
stopped by now and as it was starting to get a
light, we could see Anglesey in the distance.
However, our mistake was in trying to get back
onto the A55. We missed the sign completely and
followed a minor road virtually all the way
into Conway before we could rejoin our intended
route causing us to lose time and putting us
behind schedule. We arrived at Benllech, found
our accommodation where we were to leave the
car, changed into the walking gear and ran up
the road just as the bus flashed by. We'd missed
it and there wasn't another bus for an hour.
However, undaunted, we decided to reverse our
plan, namely to walk from Benllech to Menai
Bridge and catch a bus back at teatime.

So the venture to walk the coastline of Wales
began from Benllech beach at 8.20am on Saturday
7th October 1989. We were on our way.

The first three miles crossed the sands of Red
Wharf Bay. Fortunately the tide was out so it
was firm sand all the way. We were feeling quite
elated now as we strode out. Eventually the
beach ran out and as there is no cliff path round
Penmon Head, we took to a lane that climbed quite
steeply past the radio mast and now we were on
minor roads, all the time trying to keep as near
to the sea as possible even though we could'nt
see it. Just past Llangoed we followed a track
through a wooded area that brought us onto a
road then across scrub and shingle to the edge
of the Menai Straits. It was a good spot to stop
for lunch.

As we sat there, we realised how much we were enjoying our first experience of coastal walking. We'd made pretty good progress too, as the strongish wind had been right behind us from Benllech so missing the bus and reversing the walk had been a bonus after all. We even had a paddle in the cold sea before setting off again, but really this was a bit silly as we hadn't any towels to dry our feet properly. Looking at the map, we then realised we shouldn't have gone through the wood earlier, and so to get to Penmon we had to backtrack along the coast road, through Penmon Priory and across a field to join a lane at the tiny village of Caim. We rang Jean and Norma from a call-box to find it was raining hard at both Stoke and Loughborough. so we'd done well with the weather after all. Even a weak sun was trying to break through.

After a mile or so, the lane eventually joined back with the coast road which led into Beaumaris. Here we had an afternoon stop for a pot of tea and a teacake from a sea front cafe. and even bought some Welsh fudge for Jean and Norma.

Then we were on the last three mile flat stretch to Menai. This bit wasn't too pleasant with Saturday afternoon shoppers making the road very busy as they returned from mainland Bangor and for much of the way there was no footpath. We reached Menai Bridge and that was the end of our first walk and a new experience.

We found the bus stop we needed and fortunately didn't have too long a wait, but when the bus arrived it was packed with people wedged in like sardines. We had to stand all the way and the rucksacks were something of a hindrance to those trying to get past us in the aisle when they were getting off. Anyway all the locals were in a friendly mood and we had a good laugh.

During the day's walk, we were visualising what our B&B hosts would be like. With a name of Evans, almost certainly, we guessed, they would be Welsh, but we couldn't have been further from the truth. In fact they were Lancashire folk from just outside Manchester, having early retired to Anglesey. Introducing themselves as Bob and Val, they warmly welcomed us to their lovely bungalow. B&B accommodation was relatively new to them, but they were very accomplished and perfect hosts.

After a shower and change, we were served an absolutely gorgeous meal, three courses of home cooking for £5.00, with B&B at £11.00 that can't be bad. We went out for a quick drink at the pub but didn't stay long and soon we were back for a welcome bed and a chance to reflect on the day.

We'd been up early, driven about 120 miles in poor weather, walked 18 miles and found a super place to stay. Were we game for another 800 miles or so of Welsh coastline? . . . you bet we were.

Red Wharf Bay

Dave having a rest at Beaumaris

Day 2 Amlwch to Benllech 15 miles

After the exertions of our first day, naturally we slept like logs. We wakened with feet just a little tender and joints slightly stiff, but not too bad really. And to make matters even better, it was much nicer weather today with a clear blue sky and only a slight breeze, just about perfect conditions for walking.

Bus services on Anglesey are virtually non-existent on Sunday with just two buses all day on our route. If we could have walked from Benllech and guaranteed to reach Amlwch by 2.30, there was a bus to return us to the car, but it would have been very chancy to think we could do the fifteen miles in about four and a half hours. We had considered the idea of getting a taxi, but this was brushed aside by Bob and Val who wouldn't hear of it and insisted on taking us in their car, and we didn't really argue.

After a hearty breakfast we were on our way armed with a lunchbox prepared by Val. They dropped us off at Amlwch Port, and in case they were out when we got back at teatime, we promised we would be back to stay with them on our next visit to Anglesey, probably in the Spring.

We were really looking forward to today's walk as it promised to be mostly on the coastal cliff path rather than the lanes and roads of yesterday.

From Amlwch towards the lighthouse at Point Lynas

After leaving the tiny harbour, we were immediately climbing up onto the coast path getting glorious views down the coastline in both directions. Just past the lighthouse at Point Lynas, we had to go slightly inland for a short while in lanes which eventually led down to the sands at Dulas. A couple of young boys out on their bikes accompanied us as far as the beach asking us about walking the Welsh coastline, we replying as if we had vast experience. We didn't tell them that we only started yesterday.

In the pleasant sunshine we felt really good, and enjoyed Val's lunchbox as we sat in a clearing once off the beach. Then it was on to Lligwy, a long stretch of sand forming part of Dulas Bay, walking in the soft sand dunes. We were soon back on the coast path once more on a lovely stretch of low cliffs which took us into the pleasant village of Moelfre, passing the Lifeboat Station on the way. As we had made such good time, we decided to call in Ann's Pantry, a quaint little cafe, for a pot of tea and something to eat, wondering if hardened walkers should really be stopping for pots of tea. We think not and from here on we would concentrate on the walking.

Lligwy Beach

Looking towards Moelfre

It was just a short stroll to the next bay, Traeth Buchan, but unfortunately the tide was in and it prevented us from crossing to the next headland via the beach, so this meant a detour and a short walk along the main road before returning to the cliff path to take us into Benllech. We'd completed our weekend walking.

Back at the B&B, Bob and Val were in and we had a chat over a cup of tea before setting off, reiterating our promise to be back. As we travelled, we thought about our weekend with a difference. With hardly any ill effects, just a couple of blisters, we had achieved our intended goal and thoroughly enjoyed ourselves. There was no doubt in our minds, we'd walk the coastline of Wales no matter how long it would take us, God willing.

Traeth Buchan

Approaching Benllech

CHAPTER TWO

March 1990

Day 3 Valley to Amlwch 22 miles

This time, we decided we would definitely get the bus first out to Valley crossroads and walk back to the car. However, as with the first walk in October, getting to Anglesey wasn't without problems. We took a wrong turning just before Tarporley and ended up nearly in Whitchurch, miles off course. We recovered well though, finding an alternative road and belted into Amlwch with about five minutes spare to catch the bus. There was no leisurely breakfast this time with sandwiches and coffee being gulped down as we were flying over Britannia Bridge on to Anglesey. We'll get this travelling right one of these days.

Leaving the car on the car park at Amlwch, we had a pleasant journey to Valley on the bus. This took a little longer than the time-table showed, as the driver was making his first run on this route under the guidance of a supervisor. Anyway, he got us there.

As we left Valley in a fairly strong wind for the first section of the walk along the main road, we were stopped by a local out with his dog. He asked where we were walking to. We told him Amlwch. He said it was a long way. Yes, we agreed, we'd just come from there on the bus. He gave us a funny look, shook his head and carried on convinced he'd just met a couple of idiots. Never mind eh.

We always knew at the planning stage of the walks that we would be bound to make mistakes. If we did we would have to learn from them and make sure we didn't repeat them. At the next village, we made one such mistake.

We had decided on this trip to buy food and drink instead of preparing our own before leaving Stoke, so we stopped at Llanynghenedl newsagents to get a selection of baps and a couple of bottles of milk. It took ages to sort out—did we want mustard on the ham . . . or was it stuffing with the chicken . . . or something on the beef . . . ? It was all very confusing for us and even more for the old chap on the till when he came to price the items, but the most annoying thing about this was that, without realising it, it had taken us half an hour. You can walk about one and a half miles in that time. We had learned our lesson, never to buy food again or go in shops.

After about five miles of road walking to Llanfaethlu, the route headed left out towards the coast in lanes and eventually onto the shoreline for a pleasant section to the northern part of the island, travelling on a path above a lovely stretch of beach at Church Bay and on by the woods near Carmel Head arriving at Cemlyn Bay in the shadow of Wylfa, a nuclear power station, with quite a few people at the Visitor Centre.

After lunch, sitting on a grassy bank at the power station, the afternoon stretch took us through Cemaes Bay, a lovely little place, and eventually over many fields running parallel to the sea, where we often confused sheep tracks with trodden footpaths. We were now noticing the light was fading fast and decided in the interests of safety to abandon the path at Bull Bay and head towards Amlwch along the main road. This meant that the section between Bull Bay and Amlwch Port had been missed out, and we couldn't have that, so this short walk would have to be done at another time before we left Anglesey. This was really annoying and we were paying the penalty for messing about at the shop in the morning.

At least at the end of this walk today we had the car to take us to Benllech instead of waiting around for a bus. Val and Bob warmly greeted us again and another lovely meal was waiting for us after showering and a change into crisp, clean clothes. All this walking gives you a great appetite. Bob and Val were very interested in where we had been walking, as they too would like to try short stretches of them at some time.

We slipped out for a quick tipple after the meal, but we didn't stay too long. We needed to get back and make preparations for tomorrow's walk.

Day 4 Valley to Valley via Treaddur Bay 14 miles

There were no signs of stiffness or aches this morning, we must be getting fitter. After a full breakfast we were ready to tackle the day's stage.

Today was to be a circular walk that would take in the northern half of Holy Island, which although is still Anglesey, is connected by two bridges.

Unfortunately, we were somewhat unlucky with the weather. Although it was nice and dry with no rain forecast all day, Anglesey was caught in a cold northerly airstream, while mainland Britain was promised a day of warm sunshine.

We left the car parked at Valley crossroads and walked the three miles along the A55 into Holyhead. From what we saw of it, Holyhead was a very disappointing town, rather drab and many of the places around the docks area are definitely in need of a lick of paint.

It was a bit better further on after leaving the harbour area and it was here we stopped to meet up with some of Dave's family who had come over for a day out. There was daughter Kim and husband Dave, son Phil with wife Sally, plus Dave's dog Gemma. We met up and after a warm drink, which was very welcome, we arranged to regroup at South Stack lighthouse at lunchtime.

Continuing the walk we headed out towards Holyhead Mountain, a rather grandiose description of a large hill really, the highest point of Anglesey. For the first couple of miles, we had an easy gradual climb, but then as we began to ascend more steeply, several paths opened up. Unfortunately, we decided to take the extreme one, that is the one nearest the sea thinking it would lead us round the side of the mountain.

The path seemed to vanish gradually into nothing as the ascent became almost vertical in parts as we struggled to grab hold of any form of hand hold as we passed above North Stack on the rocky cliffs. What made things worse was the near gale force wind which was to tear the walking map from Dave's grasp and it whistled past my head into the sea. Eventually, after a final scramble over rocks, we made it onto a proper path and we found ourselves not too far from the top, with the rocks just little dots below and an angry sea even further down. We weren't half pleased to get this section behind us, after all we're supposed to be walkers, not climbers.

There were several paths to choose from at the top, and this time fortunately, we picked the right one and dropped down the steep slopes to join the approach road to South Stack lighthouse and our second meeting of the day with the family. Dave Pye looked particularly cute in his earmuffs, while Sally was bemoaning the fact, as she sat shivering in the coldish wind, that she could have been getting a sun tan in the garden back at Leicester. Still, the picnic they had brought was not to be sneezed at with just about enough food to have fed a small army.

After lunch, Dave and I carried on, leaving the others at South Stack and we'd see them later. We walked mostly on road as the coastal path is not continuous, having a short break at the small beach of Porthdafarch before arriving at Treaddur Bay meeting the kids again. They dropped Gemma off with us and it was nice to walk her for the last couple of miles as we left Holy Island via Four Mile Bridge. We returned to Valley crossroads where the family were parked, still tucking into the picnic, and even then there was still food to take back. Having said our farewells, we headed home.

Even though we had missed out on the good weather, nevertheless it had been once again a good weekend and in the end quite an exciting one with the mountain bit. The walks themselves had not been particularly attractive, but they had to be done and we looked forward to more in the summer.

CHAPTER THREE

June 1990

Day 5 Newborough to Valley 19 miles

It was a beautiful morning as we drove down to
the little town of Llangefni, oddly enough the
capital of Anglesey, not Holyhead as you would
imagine.

This time there were no hitches on the way,
and we arrived by 7.30 enabling us to get free
parking as the car-park kiosk had not yet opened,
although the town itself was getting quite active
with the market traders preparing their stalls
for the day. We changed ready for walking on the
car-park so as to be prepared to walk as soon
as we reached our destination, Newborough. The
bus took us out there and we dropped off on the
outskirts of the village.

Walking back along part of the road we had just
travelled down, we passed Newborough Forest
before bearing off towards the river estuary
at Malltraeth Sands. This was a short stretch
before a track led us away from the bay and into
a lane which eventually joined the road at the
village of Hermon. Fortunately there was very
little traffic about being so early, so walking
on the lanes and roads wasn't too bad. After
Hermon we made our way down to Aberffraw. Here

the path took us onto low cliffs and it was a pleasant two mile stretch before the track turned away from the clifftop and we were forced to take to the country lanes once more. It was so enjoyable walking in the warm sunshine and we felt really good. Now we were back on the main road into Rhosneigr, which by now was getting very busy with holidaymakers and day trippers arriving to enjoy the glorious weather.

It was getting very hot by now, and as it was getting close to lunchtime, we thought of calling for a cooling pint of shandy, but as we hadn't passed a pub and didn't want to start ambling around trying to find one, we settled for a can from the local off-licence. Note, by the way, how quickly we'd broken our vow made on our last weekend regards calling in shops. Although not particularly cold, the drink was wolfed down with lunch in the sand-dunes of Rhosneigr beach.

Resuming after lunch, the afternoon session took us along the long stretch of flat beach with the firm sand very easy to walk on. The beach, really crowded today, eventually petered out as we approached the next headland close to the airfield at RAF Valley. After a short rest on the beach, we headed round the perimeter fence of the airfield before entering fields that were to take us onto the next beach with Rhoscolyn headland beckoning. We had hoped to be able to get to Rhoscolyn on Holy Island directly by crossing the estuary instead of going back into Treaddur Bay via Valley village, but after wasting an hour trying to cross the deep mud flats of the estuary without success, we decided to retrace our steps and cut across the fields which brought us out onto the road. We found the bus-stop for our connection to return us to Llangefni.

From there it was back by car to Val and Bob's once again. We were getting to know them very well by now, which was just as well, as on this occasion they had overbooked the bungalow, and not wanting to let us down, they asked us to pose as relatives and eat in their back room to avoid the other guests. This was no hardship and we felt really at home, ending the day with the usual high standard dinner. We even had their bedroom and they slept in a caravan in the back garden. They really are such lovely people and have added to the the enjoyment of our venture.

Day 6 Bull Bay to Amlwch Port 1 mile

Treaddur Bay to Rhoscolyn 11 miles

There was no great hurry today to get on the move, as this was to be a relatively easy day's walking.

After breakfast, at which incidentally, Bob nicked our toast to give to the 'proper guests' as he put it, we drove up to Amlwch to complete the Bull Bay to Amlwch Port section which we had missed out on Day 3. It was on the way there that we dreamed up the idea of having a weekly bet on the horses. Ringing each other every Saturday would keep us in regular touch and the chance to have a natter. We would have a 'kitty' which we would regularly top up, and any returns would go towards paying our running costs on these walking weekends . . . . but more of this later.

Again the weather was very good to us and we quickly walked the one mile stretch from Bull Bay before driving down to Treaddur Bay, arriving there towards lunchtime. As the sea-front area was quite crowded and busy, we decided to move up onto the cliffs where we found a good place among the rocks to stop and eat whilst enjoying excellent views all round the bay.

Eventually, after walking about a mile and a half, we had to leave the clifftop path. It was a pity that the cliff track didn't appear to carry on all the way to Rhoscolyn and we didn't want to end up on a walk where we had to return along the same route, so we diverted into yet more country lanes and fields. We were a little over cautious in one field when our not too brilliant eyesight indicated to us that the animals in it were bulls. Carefully skirting round the outside of the field and climbing over a barbed wire fence, we were feeling very embarassed when a group of young children walked straight between the beasts a few minutes later. Obviously they weren't bulls, just biggish heifers.

Our next gaffe occured almost immediately afterwards. We spotted a path in a woodland and felt justified in scaling the wire surround fence instead of carrying on to an official path just further on. After ploughing through the undergrowth to get onto the path, getting well and truly scratched in the process, we were suddenly confronted by a chap who pointed out that we were on the private land of the Bodier Hall estate. We did a little bit of bluffing, albeit rather unconvincing, saying we were using an old map and thought that the track was a public right of way. Anyway, we apologised and he was okay about it. He even directed us on how to get out of the estate in the direction we were travelling when he could have easily asked us to retrace our steps and find another way round the headland.

From there it was just a short distance back to the clifftop through the caravan park and a return to the car at Treaddur for a quick bite before setting off for home.

This was a cracking weekend with the good weather making it all so enjoyable. One more day's walking would finish off Anglesey and then we'd be continuing our journey on mainland Wales. We had noted, incidentally, that just before finishing the day's walk, we could congratulate ourselves on the completion of the first one hundred miles of the venture, but there was still a long way to go but our minds were well focussed on our intention.

CHAPTER FOUR

October 1990

Day 7 Newborough to Menai Bridge
18 miles

This weekend would hopefully see us complete Anglesey on the Saturday, and as the bus service is so poor on Sunday for the particular section we wanted to walk on the mainland, some other transport would be necessary and so, for the first time, but certainly not the last, in stepped Norma and Jean to accompany us as the back-up team.

It was a beautiful Autumn morning as we arrived at Malltraeth, parking by the bridge while we had our breakfast. Jean and Norma couldn't have had a better introduction to our walking project. A short drive took us to Newborough forest where we left the car parked in a lay-by, and the four of us walked together for about three miles through the woods. This was very pleasant with the early morning sun and the heavy dew on the grass making a lovely picture. At one point we were able to leave the woodland path and take to the long stretch of sands before returning to the forest where we parted company with Norma and Jean, who we would now refer to as 'the girls'. They were to make their way to the car and off to spend the day doing their own thing. It was to become for them, the start of an exploration of coastal Wales having adventures of their own.

For us though there was still the walking to be done and we continued, having arranged to meet the girls at Menai Bridge around teatime. Once out of the forest, a track took us onto the main road at Dwyran where we got totally confused as we weren't able to cross reference our walking map path with the road we were on. It then dawned on us that the road was newly built and not indicated on the map. Thrown off completely, it was with some difficulty, trying farm fields and tracks, before we finally managed to get back on to our intended route as we headed towards the Menai Straits.

We stopped for lunch near to Maes Mor farm and then it was down to the water's edge of the Straits. There was a stretch then on a tarmac path that continued for about a mile or so before leading onto a shingle beach. However, this was to disappear quite quickly as the water which was rising cut off further progress and we were forced to cut inland near to Brynsiencyn, skirting fields before reaching a track that was to take us back to the main road at Llanfairpwllgwyngyll.

Since leaving the woods back at Newborough, the last few miles had been messy, that is, we were never sure exactly which path we were following. It was rather a case of trying a route and if it didn't look right, go back and try again. We must have spent about an hour of the day in total, just stopping to study the map.

However, once we were on the main road we couldn't go wrong. It was flat and straight to lead into

Menai, passing the National Trust owned, Plas Newydd, on the way.

We met the girls at the bridge and after a short stop for a drink we were on our way to Bob and Val for the last time. Although this was Jean and Norma's first visit, they thoroughly approved our choice of accomodation, and were like us, made to feel at home.

Approaching Menai Bridge

It was lovely that evening as we sat having a drink at the pub, to talk non-stop of the day's experiences with our 'new arrivals'. They could see how enthusiastic we were about this walking business and obviously, they too would become a big part of it.

Day 8 Trefor to Morfa Nefyn 10 miles

We were a long time getting started this morning as the girls spent ages nattering with Val. We finally said our goodbyes to Bob and Val with our promise that we would one day return to visit them when the walk was over. It was sad in a way to leave them as they'd been so kind and helpful to us, and we often reflected as we walked that had we had a poor B&B on our first weekend, we could well have been put off our venture. However, leave them we did and drove over to the mainland and headed for Trefor.

Trefor is a small village just over twenty miles from Bangor. We chose this starting point for two reasons. Firstly, in the walking time available, we would be able to reach Morfa Nefyn, a convenient place to meet up with Norma and Jean, and secondly for the next walk, there was a bus connection from Trefor to take us back towards Caernarvon and the north Wales coast-. We'd picked up something to have for lunch which we ate in the car, and then we were ready for the next stage.

On leaving the village, the path was not too easy to find at first, but once we did find it, we were faced immediately with a very steep climb almost reaching the top of Yr Eifl, known as 'The Rivals'. These are twin peaks of rocky cliffs about 1850 feet high, almost small mountains, with the old quarry workings still visible at the top. The track, often indistinguishable at times, took us past quite a few derelict farms and smallholdings, on terrain that was a mixture of fern, gorse, heather and rock. It was hard work but the views looking back down the coast

towards Caernarvon and the Menai Straits were
magnificent. Eventually the ground levelled out
onto a tarmac road which is used for visitors
from nearby Llithfaen to lead to a local beauty
spot and picnic area. Picnics weren't for us
though. A five minute stop for a chocolate bar
was all we could find time for, but at least it
gave us chance to get our breath back after the
exertions of the climbing.

Passing through Llithfaen, the track continued
over fields, one in particular causing us some
annoyance, as one farmer had barb-wired a gap in
the stone wall. We would have been well within
our rights to have cut the wire had it been
possible as this was a public right of way.
Anyway, we managed to scale a gate further up
the field and we were able to continue. The path
left the clifftop fields and led into Pistyll on
the main road which we followed for over a mile
into the popular seaside village of Nefyn.

The last stretch of the day took us back on the
clifftop path which joins Nefyn to Morfa Nefyn
about a mile further on, ending at the Ty Coch
beach, where we could see Jean and Norma from
a distance. They had really enjoyed themselves
in the afternoon visiting Llanbedrog on the
southern part of the peninsula. Llanbedrog is an
old haunt of Jean and I, having spent a dozen
holidays there over the years, but Norma had
never been.

We had a quick drink and a slice of Norma's
home-made date and walnut cake and then it
was time for home after a very successful and
satisfying weekend.

We'd need two more walks, which we could manage by using local bus transport for link-ups, to finish the Lleyn peninsula, and then we would need the girls for the rest of the project.

CHAPTER FIVE

March 1991

Day 9 Morfa Nefyn to Whistling Sands 16 miles

This weekend, because of the times of the buses, to walk the intended twenty one miles to Aberdaron, a very early start was required. We needed to be walking by 7.30am by the latest.

We decided therefore, instead of setting off from Stoke very early, we would travel down on the Friday evening and sleep in the car. Then first thing on Saturday we could drive the short distance to Morfa Nefyn, walk to Aberdaron and get buses back, one from Aberdaron to Pwllheli and a second from Pwllheli to Morfa Nefyn. It sounds complicated but isn't really, it's all part of the planning.

Having driven out to a lay-by just on the outskirts of Caernarvon, we parked the car and, by 11pm, we had settled down for a night's sleep, or so we thought. Disaster! The dazzle of car headlights coming from the opposite direction plus the noise of the traffic prevented us from getting off to sleep early, and as the night progressed, the uncomfortable position we were in didn't help either, so we just cat-napped. Not surprisingly we were a bit under the weather by morning and quite frankly not in the best of condition to be tackling a long walk. By 4.30am, we decided enough was enough, so we ate our bacon butties and decided to get on with it. We had set off by 5.00am and, just before 6.00am, we had parked the car by the Golf Club, and set off from the Ty Coch beach to head across Morfa Nefyn golf links.

With not feeling too brilliant, particularly as I was physically sick and had a blinding headache, early progress was slow, but eventually after two or three hours we were feeling a bit more like it and were walking reasonably although we were both tired. Unfortunately, although we improved, the weather got worse and black clouds were racing in. By mid morning the rain had started and as it turned out was to last nearly all day. Walking was now becoming increasingly difficult and dangerous as the coastal path was getting slippery and streams we had to cross were turning into miniature rivers. Stepping stones were quite immersed and our feet were getting soaked.

We managed to have a very damp lunch huddled behind a clump of rocks just short of Whistling Sands beach and decided it would be prudent to get away from the cliff path and take to the inland lanes. In any case, the walking map had by now become just a soggy mass of paper and totally unreadable. We headed south of Llangwynnadl and followed a series of lanes eventually arriving at the main Pwllheli to Aberdaron road.

By the time we had reached Aberdaron, we were thoroughly soaked to the skin and the rucksacks felt like a ton weight on our backs. The really

annoying thing about all this was that what
should have been one of the most scenic walks
we had tackled up to now had turned out to be a
total washout, and what made it worse was that
we would have to link up the Whistling Sands to
Aberdaron section on a future walk. Still, we
knew that we would get these sort of setbacks
when we were at the planning stage of these
walks, so we'd just put it behind us and get
on with it without moaning and hope we wouldn't
have too many bad weather days.

Because of curtailing today's walk, as we had
quite a bit of time to spare in Aberdaron before
our bus was due, we finished the day off with a
gorgeous pot of tea and a bowl of hot soup in the
little beach cafe, which was really just about
the best thing of the day.

The bus took us to Pwllheli where we were to get
our next connection. There was sufficient time
to get provisions for Sunday's walk. This was
a first for us preparing our own lunch, as Val
had done the first three weekends and the girls
doing the others. Arriving back in Morfa Nefyn,
we picked up the car and made our way to the
Brigadoon hotel.

By now the rain had stopped and the Sunday
weather forecast was looking much better. The
hotel itself left something to be desired but
the evening dinner and breakfast next morning
couldn't be faulted. After a wet and exhausting
day we were shattered, and by 9.00pm. we had
flaked out.

Day 10 Trefor to Bontnewydd 15 miles

When we planned the walks originally, we had decided that we would not follow each stage in sequence, that is, we wouldn't necessarily start the next point where we had left off the last. Due to a shortage of daylight hours, early Spring and late Autumn walks would have to be the more accessible ones nearer home, so we felt now was the time to be thinking of tackling the ninety five miles of the north Wales section. Today's walk therefore, was to start heading us back in that direction and then with this out of the way, we could manage the remaining eighty or so miles in two weekends.

We woke completely refreshed with no after effects or even thoughts of yesterday's fiasco, and after a good breakfast we were raring to go.

The walking gear which, thanks to the Brigadoon's hot radiators, had dried out nicely after yesterday's soaking was packed and we drove out to Trefor village once again. After parking the car, we were soon heading north westerly.

The weather was much better today and although dull, at least it wasn't raining. Walking today was very ordinary with not a cliff in sight as we headed along the A499 for about eight miles passing through Clynnog Fawr and Pontlyfni. Clynnog Fawr, a village of whitewashed cottages, has one of the best known churches in Wales. It was founded by St.Beuno in the 7th century and became a stopping place for pilgrims on the way to Bardsey Island. Eventually we veered off down a lane to take us to the sea at Dinas Dinlle, arriving just at lunchtime. We sat at a broken picnic bench to eat on the sandy beach, in fact all the picnic benches were broken, and Dinas Dinlle is supposed to be a 'blue flag' category award beach, but we couldn't agree with this, certainly not from what we saw of it.

After lunch we continued round to Caernarvon Airport. It's not possible to get right to the end of the airfield so we had to cut across this section and then followed a track which led to a girdered footbridge over the river. The bridge was in about the same state as the picnic benches and we almost did the splits as we stretched across a missing section. It had started to drizzle by now but it didn't last too long, and carrying on a series of lanes took us into the village of Bontnewydd. Our timing was good and we didn't have too long to wait for the bus to get us back to Trefor.

The Brigadoon had fixed us up with a flask of hot water to make a drink, so after a warming coffee, we were ready for home.

This had been quite a mixed weekend. We were disappointed about not reaching Aberdaron by the intended route, but at least we'd got the Sunday walk just perfect and this meant we could look forward to doing the north Wales section in Autumn this year and Spring next year.

CHAPTER SIX

June 1996

Day 11 Pwllheli to Aberdaron 20 miles

Earlier in the year, the four of us had a short holiday in the Lake District. On a trip into Grasmere, we saw a sign in a shop, "Hiking poles—£10 each or £19 for two!". We'd got most of the necessary gear, good comfortable boots, quality waterproof coats, overtrousers, gaiters and pedometers. The hiking poles would be the finishing touch, so we bought them. We tried them out on a short walk round the roads and hills in the area. There was a sharp click as the metal spike of the pole touched the walking surface.

Now, being in Wordsworth country, we felt in a poetic mood, and our new poles or sticks inspired us to verse . . . .

THE CLICK OF THE STICK

The click of the stick, the wait at the gate,
Who's that on the path, just me and my mate.
The click of the stick, the pee at the tree,
Shall we make it, we'll just have to see.
The click of the stick, the stop at the shop,
It sometimes gets tough, but we'll walk till we drop.

The click of the stick, a monotonous sound,
Silence is broken when we're around.
It drives you crazy, it gets on your wick,
When all you can hear, is the click of the
stick.

G.Bell & D. Pridmore

(Last of the Lakeland poets)

After that bit of daft, back to the
walk . . . .

In actual fact, with regard to the sticks, we
don't need them yet with lots of flat walking to
get on with, but they'll certainly be an asset
when we reach the steep hills and valleys of the
Pembrokeshire Coast Path.

What a difference in the weather from the last
time we were in Pwllheli. Today it was clear
blue sky with hardly any breeze, and it promised
to be very warm later. We had arrived by 7.0am
and there was plenty of time to enjoy a casual
breakfast before setting off.

A bit of shingle beach took us along the first
stretch towards Penrhos walking parallel to the
golf course which was quite busy even so early
in the morning. There was some scrambling over
rocks to get us over a small headland and onto the
long stretch of soft sand of Llanbedrog beach.
As the tide was in, access to the clifftop path
was out, so we had to leave the beach and follow
a lane to skirt the headland, known locally as
'the Aggie'. This path led us onto another long
sandy stretch, the Warren beach which serves the
holidaymakers from the huge caravan park. The

sand here was much firmer making progress much easier.

Soon we were in Abersoch and made our way round the harbour to reach the west shore beach which was already beginning to get quite busy. After a short stop we pushed on until the beach ran out and we were forced to take to a lane which in turn led to a public footpath across fields—we nearly missed this one. The signpost was well hidden in the overgrown hedge and it was as well we spotted it, otherwise we could have been heading back to Abersoch via a different route.

There were several small fields to negotiate before finally reaching the grassy hill which overlooked 'Hell's Mouth' or Porth Neigwl to give it it's proper name. This was yet another long stretch of sand, about three miles long in fact. We walked half way along the beach before deciding to stop. In the pleasant sunshine it was very relaxing to stretch out and eat our lunch.

After lunch we completed the rest of the beach and joined a road. This climbed quite steeply as we approached the village of Rhiw and it was hard work in the hot sun particularly straight on top of lunch. Once through Rhiw, the road narrowed considerably and took us on a gradual slope into Aberdaron. Just before reaching the promenade, we met the floats of the local carnival parade. Everyone seemed to be enjoying themselves, and like us, were appreciating the good weather.

Relaxing on Aberdaron beach

We had made such good time today that we were able to take an ice cream onto the sands and enjoy a bit of sunbathing while we were waiting for the bus to return us to Pwllheli. Having picked up the car, we drove to Abersoch to find the Ty Draw guest house, our B&B accommodation.

Unfortunately, we were unable to get a meal at the B&B, so we ended up at the Ship Inn at Llanbedrog for our food. It ended what had been a good and satisfying day.

Day 12 Aberdaron to Whistling Sands 11 miles

The Ty Draw accommodation was very much a big disappointment especially considering it was the most expensive we'd stayed in so far. It lacked the homeliness and atmosphere of Val and Bob's even the less salubrious Brigadoon. The owners were friendly but we felt a bit second rate to the full-board guests.

Anyway we got a good night's sleep but were wakened by the sound of rain on the skylight. This was a bit of a turn up particularly after the glorious weather of yesterday, but only to be expected from past experiences of the Lleyn peninsula. The weather can be very changeable probably due to the mountainous nature of the area. Breakfast was only ordinary but nevertheless filling, and soon we were on our way to Aberdaron where we parked the car.

Besides the rain, what a contrast in temperature and we certainly put behind us any ideas of walking in shorts. However by the time we'd got the gear on, the rain had actually stopped and we were off on the coastal path which was accessed from the beach.

This was a good section with a well maintained path and we were enjoying it. We even had a few patches of blue sky and a hazy sun was trying to get through.

The path divided after a while and we dropped down onto the rocks of Bardsey Sound, a two mile wide strip of water dividing the mainland from Bardsey Island. We were disgusted with ourselves when we had to climb back up to our original high-level path a few minutes later and another lesson was learned from this which we would apply for all future walks—if there was a choice of paths, we'd always stick to the higher.

After crossing a couple of stone walled fields we reached the tip of the peninsula where the path turned slightly inland although still in view of the sea. Then we were faced with a long, steep grassy slope which emerged onto a road. We were now at Mynydd Mawr, a hill about 520ft above sea level. A rough track led from the road to cut across the headland although this wasn't too easy to find at first. On the other side of the hill we were on, was a track that returned to sea level where it is possible to visit St. Mary's Well which pilgrims to Bardsey drank from as they waited for a boat to the island.

The path through masses of ferns was quite easy to walk and soon we joined up with the road taking us to Whistling Sands car park, although we didn't carry on right down to the beach. From here it was just a matter of returning to Aberdaron by the shortest route having satisfied ourselves that we had completed the missed link of the coastline. Returning quickly was necessary anyway as it had started to rain heavily again and we were getting rather wet. It's marvellous that the two occasions we'd visited Whistling Sands, we'd had a soaking.

We got out of the wet gear back at the car park, drove a couple of miles up the road and had a late lunch. There was a ten minute rest and then it was time for home.

CHAPTER SEVEN

October 1991

Day 13 Pwllheli to Harlech 26 miles

Again it was back to Pwllheli sea front by 7.30am, and lovely to have the girls with us once more. It didn't seem twelve months since their last trip with us. They were just as keen, if not keener than us, and the early start didn't bother them at all. They would be providing the transport on all the walks from now on.

There was the usual bacon sandwich breakfast and then all four of us set off in lovely Autumn weather walking round by the Marina and onto the sands of Abererch beach. We took to the dunes after a couple of miles as Norma and Jean wanted to get a bus from Butlin's Holiday Camp. A track eventually led inland and onto the main road and the perimeter fence of the camp. Leaving them to wait for the bus to take them back to the car at Pwllheli we carried on staying mainly on the main road, but this wasn't too bad as the grass verge was quite wide in parts.

Just before reaching Llanystumdwy, the village where the former Liberal Prime Minister, David Lloyd George, grew up and spent his life, we followed a lane leading towards the sea. The intention was to walk down the western side of the tidal estuary formed by the confluence of the Rivers Dwyfor and Dwyfach and cross the estuary by a bridge. Unfortunately for us, the bridge had been destroyed in storms some few years earlier, but our old map didn't show it. We'd walked about half an hour before finding out, and we were forced to retrace our steps, and although we climbed the railway embankment and walked along the track to get over the water instead of returning to the main road, nevertheless we had put an extra two to three miles on our journey. This was so frustrating as today's walk was a long one.

Soon we arrived in Criccieth passing the ruins of the 13th century Castle on the towering headland. We followed the beach road through the town and walked alongside the fenced-off railway line for about a mile. When the track turned inland, we continued on a more undefined path over a craggy headland to drop down onto Morfa Bychan beach, more commonly known as Black Rock Sands and here seemed a good place to stop for lunch.

It was very pleasant walking along the sands after we had eaten, but then we were forced to follow the road through the caravan park for a short way before we rejoined the coast path near the golf course. We climbed steadily into a lane which then led back down to the sea front at Borth-y-Gest. A legend which upsets the history books is attached to this quiet village, for it is said that it was from here that Prince Madog set sail to discover America—more than 300 years before Christopher Columbus.

Following the low level path for a mile, we emerged at the eastern end of the main street in Porthmadog, a thriving harbour town, very busy today with end of season holidaymakers and Saturday shoppers.

Between here and the 3/4 mile stretch to the toll gate there is no pavement and we had to walk this section alongside the rails of the Ffestiniog Railway, finding time to have a five minute rest near the station to take in the wonderful surrounding views of Tremadog Bay and the mountainous areas of Snowdonia inland.

By the Ffestiniog Railway

However, once past the toll, the route was far from attractive on an extremely busy main road, and it was mainly uphill too. We passed the signs for the famous "Italian" village of Portmerion but none of the paths around there were of any use to us, so we just had to stick to the road—about three miles of it. Thankfully at Penrhyndeudraeth, the sign for the Harlech Toll took us away from the road and the next stretch was much quieter.

After about a mile on this minor road passing over the toll bridge, we came to another busy A-road but fortunately we spotted a narrow track which ran alongside a ditch cutting inside the road. Soon we had lost the sight and sound of the traffic as the road and track diverged with our path entering a wooded section. It was pleasant going. As we progressed, we came across a flock of sheep wandering all over the place. Presumably they had come from one of the nearby fields. Some were on the path, others in the ditch or on the embankment, and as usual these stupid animals panicked as we approached and we found ourselves driving a lot of them ahead of us on the path. Their only way to regroup was to get back past us via the ditch which eventually they did, but nevertheless we must have herded at least half of them half a mile down the path.

Eventually we rejoined the major road and needed to make a decision. We'd told the girls, who would book a B&B while they were out on their travels, that it would be a 5.30 to 6pm finish today and that we would be 'somewhere' on the main road where they could pick us up. However, we were already running late and to stick to a coastal aspect of the walk, we were hoping to get over Morfa Harlech cliffs and finish on the beach before getting back onto the road. It would be touch and go as to whether we would make it, but decided to have a go.

There was quite a stiff climb through a couple of stone-walled fields but the route wasn't too clear when we reached a wood and we were wasting time trying to sort it out. We just couldn't risk it especially as the light was beginning to fade, so we changed our minds and moved down through Llanfihangel village on the side of the hill and we were back on the main road. Norma and Jean turned up a few minutes later having booked accommodation at "Gwrach Ynys", an isolated guest house just a couple of minutes down the road. Sadly, to order an evening meal in, it needed to have been booked by 6pm and we were just too late. Still we had a nice meal out in Harlech, reflecting that today had been our longest walk yet, thanks to the detour at Criccieth, and it turned out we were never to exceed this distance in a single day.

Day 14 Harlech to Barmouth 16 miles

Dave and I decided we would leave it to the girls to book all the B&B's from now on as the accomodation at Gwrach was absolutely brilliant, very tasteful, and we were regretting not having been in time for yesterday's evening meal which we imagined would have to a high standard if breakfast was anything to go on. Still it couldn't be helped.

It was a typical Autumn morning, very misty with a distinct chill in the air, but the weather forecast was good for later on so we weren't deterred. As our accommodation was on the main road, we were walking immediately we left the house, no need for transport to a start point.

The first three miles were on the busy road passing through Harlech town with it's castle dominating the skyline. A dirt track took us off the road to run alongside the Royal St. David's golf course for half a mile. The grass was heavy with dew, and with the sun trying to get through, the course looked very attractive especially with the backdrop of the sea and mountains. The track petered out and we had a stiffish climb to get us back onto the main road, but a mile later a sign pointed the way to Llandanwyg, a small village almost at the sea's edge. Although we couldn't get onto the beach, a path followed the banks of a small river which we crossed by walking a few hundred yards on the railway line leaving it at Llanbedr station. We headed for the tall sand dunes of Shell Island.

Shell Island is not really an island at all, but a peninsula formed originally early in the 19th century by the diverted River Artro. Because of the peculiarities of the offshore currents, this area, also called Mochras, is covered in shells of more than 200 different kinds. Sand dunes are always very difficult to negotiate as there are so many natural tracks as was the case around this area, and it took us quite some time to find our way out before joining the Llanbedr airfield perimeter fence.

Over on our right, the massive sand hills blocked any views of the sea and although we felt there would have been a walkable beach on the other side, we didn't relish the idea of trying to scale the dunes on the very soft sand. It would probably mean one yard forward and two back, really not worth the effort. An opportunity to get onto the beach would come later. This stretch of dunes is called Morfa Dyffryn, the central and northern part of which is a national nature reserve.

We kept to a flat inland route following the airfield fence for over a mile until we came to Dyffryn caravan park. This was very busy. A wide track led through the dunes onto a wide expanse of sand, and we found a nice quiet spot to stretch out and have our lunch only about fifty yards from the sea.

The weather was lovely and warm by now, perfect considering it was October and after finishing eating, we were onto the beach for the final leg of the weekend. It was easy walking on the firmish sand and we made good progress hoping to remain on the beach right the way into Barmouth, but the tide was racing in. Although we tried to make it by scrambling over rocks and even paddling with our boots slung round our necks, we were forced to look for an opportunity to get to dry land. This came at Llanaber railway station which we climbed up to and continued to Barmouth on the road.

In the fine summerlike weather, Barmouth beach and promenade was quite crowded with people making the most of what would probably be the last fling before Winter.

Jean and Norma were waiting for us and after a change of clothes and a pot of tea in one of the cafes, it was time to set off for home. It really has been a brilliant weekend and we've all enjoyed it. One thing we felt happy about was that the 42 miles we'd walked this weekend had left no ill effects, so we concluded we must be reasonably fit. We can't wait to come back next year.

CHAPTER EIGHT

June 1992

Day 15 Fairbourne to Aberystwyth 24 miles

It was a glorious Summer morning as we arrived in Fairbourne, having driven down through Bala which was a new route for us. The scenery, particularly as we passed through the Snowdonia National Park, was stunning. Obviously, by starting the walk at Fairbourne, it meant we had missed out walking the toll bridge over the River Mawddach at Barmouth and so, as with the Menai Bridge, it will have to be walked at some time in the future.

We were walking by 8am, first crossing the railway line at Mawddach station, then along the promenade. From there it was road walking on the A493 for a few miles, which wasn't too pleasant because of the busy road. Just before Rhoslefain on the sharp bend, we turned across fields ending in a lane which took us through Llanfendigaid and Tonfanau, and now we were well away from traffic. By the station, a rough track led to the large expanse of water, Broad Water, which we crossed by climbing onto the railway bridge. On the other side we dropped down onto the sands just north of Towyn, and followed this long beach through Towyn itself and then onto

Aberdovey. This section seemed to go on forever, and it was difficult to make out Aberdovey from a distance due to the sea mist and heat haze with the temperature really building up now.

At the end of the beach, Norma and Jean were waiting for us and we all had lunch together. Although the weather had been very warm, nevertheless we had only had one rest and as a result we found we had covered 16 miles. We decided this would be the policy in future—walk for at least three hours before stopping, getting about ten miles under our belts, and then afternoon walks would not have to be rushed to finish.

After lunch, Norma drove us round the Dovey estuary to Ynyslas. Dave was feeling a bit off colour and had a little doze. The Dovey estuary is a bit of a pain in the backside. The distance from the harbour at Aberdovey to Ynyslas across the river is only about a mile at the most, but there is no access across the mud flats without trespassing on the railway line. Therefore to get round the estuary you have to walk twenty two miles on a busy road that has little or no pavement for most of the way, a prospect we were not relishing. We decided on this occasion to ignore it and review the situation at a future date.

The girls dropped us off and went in search of accommodation in or around Aberystwyth. For us, once through Ynyslas, the path crossed the golf course and led onto Borth beach which by now was crowded with holidaymakers basking in the red hot sunshine. It was the heat that was making walking uncomfortable, particularly on the very steep climb out of Borth and onto the coastal path.

Things wouldn't have been quite so bad except that the stiff climbs were followed by steep descents onto small beaches and then re-ascending—a real switchback section and something we could have done without, particularly as Dave seemed to have strained his leg and he really struggled on the very steep sections. Furthermore, we were totally exposed to the sun with no shelter and we were beginning to burn. However, despite these hardships, we were rewarded with magnificent views all round Cardigan Bay.

Needless to say, we stopped several times on this stretch taking in as much liquid as we could from the oranges we had. We reached Clarach Bay where there is a large caravan park, and for the first time since leaving Borth, we got some shelter in a wooded area, part of the park. We climbed over Constitution Hill and it was with some relief as we rounded a curve in the path, to see Aberystwyth, and we couldn't wait to get to the pier, our rendezvous point. This was probably the only time of the whole walk that we wanted to get it over with. Having walked twenty four miles in blistering heat, we were exhausted.

Aberystwyth viewed from Constitution Hill

Jean came to meet us having left Norma at the accommodation they had booked, "Llwynygog", a guest house kept by a sweet elderly lady—Miss Pugh. She used to do B&B with her sister, but after the sister had died, she ran the place herself, really for the company. She was lovely and the house so homely and comfortable. £11.00 was all she charged—ridiculous.

We managed to find a bistro in the town for our evening meal, and in between courses we were virtually falling asleep. It had been one heck of an exhausting day.

Day 16 Aberystwyth to Aberaeron 16 miles

More lovely weather was forecast for today and over breakfast, Jean and Norma stated their plans. They were driving out to Devil's Bridge, an area of outstanding scenery, and later on they would visit the silver and lead mines at Llywernog. It sounded like a good day out.

Dave and I set off picking up a morning paper from the newsagents where the lady behind the counter, being a bit of a walker herself she said, was interested in where we were walking. She was impressed when we told her of the whole Welsh coast walk, wished us luck and even tried to teach us a few Welsh phrases which might come in useful, but we very much doubted it.

We left the town centre and hit the coastal path more or less straight away. Again there were a few switchbacks, but given that we were much fresher and also the fact that the early morning sun was giving nothing like the temperatures of yesterday, we coped with them easily. After about three miles we had to leave the coast and take to a lane which led past a radio mast. This lane joined the main road for a short while before we returned to the next section of the clifftop path, slipping and sliding through gorse and bracken as we tried to take a short cut and got ourselves well and truly scratched in the process. We had lunch surrounded by a flock of sheep who, unlike the stupid panicking beasts at Harlech, must have been used to walkers as they ignored us and just carried on grazing.

Shortly after, we came across two lovely sited caravan parks at Llanrhystud and Llansantffraid, and from there we had glorious views looking down the bay, and we could make out the headland of New Quay in the distance. Unfortunately, the coastal path petered out here and we forced back onto the main road at Llanon where we stopped for an ice cream, much needed as the weather was very warm by now.

The next stage was miserable walking. We were on an extremely busy road and the fact that there was no pavement made it quite dangerous. With only a narrow grass verge to walk on, we had several stops pressing ourselves against the hedge to avoid the speeding traffic. Eventually the road began to climb quite steeply on a winding section, and as safety barriers were in place, at least we were able to walk inside them and felt much safer. The stiff climb in the heat though had certainly made us gasp. We were now overlooking Aberarth.

At Aberarth, a small quaint village, the track to the beach passed in front of a row of terraced cottages all displaying a riot of colour from the window-boxes and hanging baskets. The locals obviously take great pride in their village.

The last mile into Aberaeron was on a very pebbly beach which eventually led onto a short promenade. The girls were there to meet us and we went to the beach cafe for a pot of tea, although the owner and his wife were cleaning up and just about ready to close for the day. The hot weather had taken more out of us than we thought and we were rather dry. When we asked for a pint of milk, they didn't have any, but the owner's young daughter, bless her, cycled to the local supermarket and brought back two bottles which we wolfed down in one swig—it was nectar.

The girls told us of their day out at Devil's Bridge seeing the Mynach Falls, followed by a visit to the silver and lead mine at Llywernog. This is a 6.5 acre open air museum where there is a rock crusher house and three working water wheels. Visitors can follow a Miner's Trail and also go underground to see the Blue Pool, a floodlit cavern. They'd really enjoyed the day.

This had been an exhausting weekend walkwise. By the time we had driven to the 'Green Dragon' pub on the outskirts of Welshpool to get an evening meal, our already aching legs were stiffening up and we crossed the car-park in some discomfort, but at least, as we looked at the map, we were encouraged to see just how far the last two weekends have 'dropped' us down the coastline as we now head for west Wales.

CHAPTER NINE

August 1992

Day 17 Aberaeron to Llangrannog 14 miles

We made very good time getting down to Aberaeron which enabled the four of us to have breakfast and a casual stroll around the harbour before getting the walking gear on. Aberaeron is a lovely little place with it's beautiful Regency houses painted in contrasting pastel shades in the harbourside streets. We all liked Aberaeron very much.

Jean and Norma decided this morning not to walk with us but would meet up with us at lunchtime in Llangrannog, our intention being to get to Cardigan by the end of the day.

We were quickly up onto the coastal path and it was a lovely stretch to walk with good views all round Cardigan Bay. The path dropped down to the road approaching New Quay and we continued on this, crossing the narrow sloping streets leading to the harbour. The building of the quay, after which the town was named in 1835, at one time provided the only safe harbour along this whole stretch of coast.

Once we'd climbed back to the high ground again, we had yet more pleasant walking on the springy turf, meeting and speaking with a Dutch couple who too were admiring the great views. We reached the point of descent to the small beach of Cwmtudu when we had a bit of a disaster.

As we were about to climb a stile, I discovered my glasses were missing from my shirt breast pocket. There was a hole in the pocket and being loose the specs had fallen through unnoticed. I didn't have any spares either with me or at home, and although I could have survived the weekend, I would certainly need them on Monday for work. There was nothing for it except to retrace our steps in the hope of finding them. We walked back towards New Quay for half an hour to more or less where we had met the Dutch people, but no luck. We gave up and headed back. Then about 50 yards from where I'd noticed the loss, I spotted something glinting on a frond of bracken—it was the specs.

For something that was only yards away, we had walked for an hour the equivalent of about three miles, and we were annoyed. We'd lost time and would be well behind our scheduled meeting with the girls—but there was still worse to come.

The path dropped down to Cwmtudu and we followed a lane which led away from the beach area. We chose the lane route as opposed to looking for the cliff path because we thought it would be less hassle and we could perhaps make up a bit of the lost time. At first the lane climbed gently but then got steeper and steeper going on for about a mile, leaving us gasping for breath. It was hard work. Then, emerging from the tree-lined route at the top of the hill, we noticed a distinct change in the weather with black clouds gathering. The rain started and in minutes was lashing down like stair rods, and with virtually nowhere to shelter except hedgerows, we were absolutely drenched in no time. Trying to get into our waterproofs was extremely difficult and in any case seemed totally pointless as we were already in sodden clothes.

The descent into Llangrannog was most unpleasant. Drains couldn't cope with the rainwater and the road quickly turned into a river as we made our way down. Because we were running late, Jean and Norma had come to look for us and nearly got stuck in the lake which had formed across the road at the bottom of the hill in Llangrannog village. This cloudburst had certainly been a nightmare.

When we arrived in the beach area, our only objective was to get out of the wet clothes which were literally stuck to us. Having changed into dry clothes with some difficulty in the public toilets, we joined the girls and the four of us had a snack in one of the cafes, and decided regretfully to abandon the walk for the day. Obviously, if we had not wasted time looking for the glasses, we would have reached Llangrannog before the storm had started, had lunch during it, and continued when the storm had ceased, which in the afternoon it did. However it was too late and we just had to accept it.

It had been the girl's intention to find a B&B during the afternoon whilst we were walking, but as we had called it a day, we all went into Cardigan town where we got fixed up through the

Tourist Information Office. The accommodation was only moderate on this occasion but at least the owner s wife said she would dry off our saturated boots in the greenhouse ready for tomorrow.

For our meal out at the local Chinese restaurant in the evening, we ordered the banquet meal for four, but couldn't finish it.

We reflected that the day had been disappointing in as much as we had only covered a short distance and wouldn't start the Pembrokeshire Coast path this weekend as we had hoped.

Day 18 St. Dogmael's to Llangrannog 15 miles

St. Dogmaels is a small village about a mile outside Cardigan and is the start of the Pembrokeshire Coastal Path. After breakfast we decided to drive to the signpost 'St. Dogmaels' and walk back through Cardigan on our way to Llangrannog, then on our next trip down we would be starting Pembrokeshire from it's border.

The guest house had made a good job of drying our wet gear from yesterday, and we were soon on our way.

The weather was very undecided this morning with the threat of rain later on, so we needed to push on to try and beat it. Unfortunately we couldn't find a way to the cliff top, in fact we weren't too sure if there was a continuous coastal path although we knew that there were good beaches on this stretch of coast, particularly at Mwnt. Anyway, because of the rain threat we decided not to waste time looking for a coast route, but to carry on along lanes and minor roads running parallel to the coast. The roads weren't too bad to walk on as there were plenty of grass verges making it much easier on the feet than concrete and tarmac.

Eventually the road led down the steep hill to arrive in the little village of Aberporth which was quite busy considering the doubtful weather. Aberporth is a pretty place with two small, sandy and well sheltered beaches separated by a headland. The road we were on just continued as part of the promenade and then turned sharply up the hill and away from the sea. We felt a few spots of rain which didn't last long, but as we approached Tresaith, the rain started again, this time more steadily. We sat by the entrance of the large caravan site sheltering under a tree to have our lunch, with the lane now becoming quite busy as people scurried back to their caravans to dodge the rain.

We carried on and for the first time today we actually saw a footpath sign that pointed towards the coast. This we followed and it was to bring us onto a track leading to the cliff top, now enshrouded in mist and low rain cloud. With an already muddy path from yesterday's cloudburst being made worse by today's rain the route was very slippery in parts and we had to take a lot of care on the descent into Llangrannog. It is a great pity that Llangrannog has welcomed us with rain twice this weekend as it is such a lovely little bay, but the weather is something we can't control.

One cheering note though—just before finishing today's walk, we passed the 300 mile mark.

Once down at the beach cafe, as there was no sight of the girls, and being in need of a nice warm drink, we left all the wet gear outside and sat waiting while we had a pot of tea. There was still no sign of them, so we had another pot of tea. At last they arrived, hungry as usual, and spotted the lemon meringue pie. So it was two slices of pie and a pot of tea for four. Dave and I had knocked up quite a bill by the time we had to set off for home.

We have been a little disappointed this weekend in that we'd come a long way to cover a relatively short distance and fallen short of our goal, but at least we'd had a lot of laughs and enjoyed ourselves. What is more, we're now in sight of Pembrokeshire and its famous Coast Path.

CHAPTER TEN

October 1992

Day 19 Bontnewydd to Penmaenmawr
23 miles

Now we were in Autumn, we thought it was time to try and finish off the north Wales section in, hopefully, two more weekends.

We drove down through Caernarvon and not surprisingly gave a little shudder as we passed the lay-by in which we had spent the night in the car back in March 1991.

Arriving in Bontnewydd we found the lane we were to start from so we had time to eat a leisurely breakfast. We left the car and the four of us walked down the lane, then onto a track taking us past a farm, and then finally continuing to join a road down at the water's edge of the Menai Straits.

Norma and Jean parted company with us at this point and returned to the car and off for their day out. They were off to Caernarvon Castle to enjoy an interesting morning there before going on to get us accommodation in the Penmaenmawr area. On the way down in the car earlier on, we had passed Penmaenmawr railway station which we thought would be a suitable place for us to meet up with in the afternoon.

In good walking weather we set off along the concrete pavement, past the already busy golf course and into Caernarvon. We negotiated the bridge by the castle and followed the road near to the Menai Straits until we were clear of the town. Bob and Val Evans, back at Benllech, had told us there was a walk along the old disused railway line. This we followed, but what they hadn't told us was that it only went on for about a mile or so, and when we reached an overgrown area and could go no further, we had to turn into a field, then climb a stone wall to bring us onto the Caernarvon to Bangor road.

This wasn't exactly exciting as we continued on this flat and uninteresting road which was quite busy. We spotted, at times, signs of the old railway line but we could see no access to it until just short of Port Dinorwic where we walked a short section before stopping for a break close to the yacht club. Then it was more road as we headed for Bangor. By this time it was getting towards lunch.

Strictly speaking, we should have headed towards the Menai Bridge on our approach to the town and kept to the outskirts following the Straits, but we ignored the sign thinking there was another further on. There wasn't, so we just continued right through the centre, very busy with Saturday morning shoppers. We threaded our way through and headed out towards the sea, approaching another road with the harbour down to our left. We were ready for lunch now and looked for somewhere to stop.

Our map indicated there were tracks off the road which would skirt Penrhyn Castle, now owned by the National Trust, but the path we found seemed more private than public, so after a quick exploration of alternatives, we gave up and decided to eat sitting on a bridge by the Penrhyn Castle grounds. At least this was off the main road.

Resuming after, we stayed on the main road climbing the hill out of Bangor before at last we saw a path leading down to the water's edge. At first we were on shingle but soon picked up a more recognizable path which we followed through Llanfairfechan until the track actually opened up onto the large expanse of sand of Penmaenmawr beach.

It was just a matter then of finding an exit off the beach to cross the road bridge over the busy A55. This brought us almost onto the railway station where we met up with the girls. We drove to our B&B accommodation at Conway which they had booked earlier having found nowhere suitable in Penmaenmawr.

Mrs. Hughes' at Berry Street was quite acceptable, but again we couldn't get an evening meal in, so it was out to Alfonso's, the local Italian restaurant, in the evening. Unfortunately, Dave didn't feel too well during the meal and went to sit outside in the fresh air leaving the three of us feeling guilty sitting tucking into our meal. Anyway the staff put the steak and sauce into a container and gave it to us for him to eat later.

Our feet were just a little sore after walking a lot of miles on tarmac today and we couldn't wait to put them up.

Day 20 Penmaenmawr to Llandudno 16 miles

After a good night's sleep, Dave was fine this morning and raring to go.

To be able to get to Conway from Penmaenmawr, you have to be lucky with the tide. If it's out you can get quite easily by staying on the beach. Needless to say, we were unlucky and it seemed at first that we faced the prospect of walking along the A55 which we quickly dismissed as being suicidal. Talking to Mrs. Hughes over a good filling breakfast, she came up with another alternative which was to climb round the back side of Conway Mountain. She said it would be hard going, but well worth it. We decided to go for this suggestion, after all anything was better than walking the A55.

We drove back towards Llanfairfechan and parked the car at the foothills of Tal-y-Fan mountain. Immediately we were able to get onto the track which ascended quite steeply onto the grassy slopes but this we didn't mind as we were miles away from the traffic and seemed to have the hills to ourselves. The views all round were terrific and the walking was getting easier once we were near the top. There we saw a walking party, probably a Ramblers Club, who had arrived via another ascent on the far side of the hill. Obviously being so high it was much cooler and there were a few spots of rain but nothing to worry about.

Mountain route to Conway

Looking towards the Sychnant Pass

It seemed a little unusual to think we were doing a coastal walk and yet here we were high in the hills with the sea only in view at a distance from time to time.

Eventually the track dropped and once out through the bracken, we found ourselves on the old Conway to Bangor road. We spotted an Austrian restaurant on the road which we noted as a possible evening meal venue on our next visit to the area. Then after a steady climb along the road, we were on the Sychnant Pass and started our descent towards Conway now visible in the distance.

High above Penmaenmawr

At last we were in Conway passing by the castle walls and carrying on through the town.

Conway is a delightful place. Obviously it's main feature is the Edward I built castle, but it has others. There are three bridges which span the Conway estuary—Telford's elegant suspension bridge opened in 1826, Stephenson's tubular railway bridge opened in 1848 and the graceful modern road bridge. Down on the quayside is what is said to be the smallest house in Britain, measuring just 6ft across and 10ft 2in to the top of it's upper storey.

After crossing the bridge, we thought it was time for lunch so with the tide being out, we managed to find a spot on the banks of the estuary at Deganwy.

We continued until we had to leave the shoreline and follow the road round by Deganwy railway station. There was a track which led into the dunes that formed part of the golf course and we followed this route all the way into Llandudno, arriving at the West Shore beach.

Conway Castle

Rock climbing on the Great Orme

As we progressed on what was a gradual slope, we came across groups of climbers who were attempting to scale the sheer rock faces of the Orme—rather them than us we felt. Eventually after levelling out at Great Orme Head, we started on the two mile descent into Llandudno with the path joining the promenade just above the pier.

There were still plenty of people out and about enjoying the Autumn sunshine in this pleasant popular seaside town, though it was now becoming much cooler towards the end of the day. We threaded our way through them on the wide promenade for the last mile, passing as we did so, the 'Glenormes Hotel' where Jean and I spent our honeymoon back in 1959. Just before reaching the Little Orme at Penrhyn-side, the girls were waiting with a welcome cup of coffee, and once we'd downed it we were ready for the journey back home.

We stopped at Abergele to get fish and chips at a shop highly recommended by Sir Harry Secombe, or so the posters on the walls of the shop said. Three of us had fish and chips, Dave just chips, but what did he have with them?—the steak a la Italian saved from last night, so it wasn't wasted after all. Well done Dave.

It's been yet again another enjoyable weekend, and we've walked sufficient miles to ensure that, barring accidents, we should be able to finish the north Wales section in one more weekend.

CHAPTER ELEVEN

March 1993

Day 21 Saughall to Prestatyn 24 miles

Probably not many people have heard of Saughall, and quite honestly until taking up this walking project, neither had we.

Saughall is a little village about six miles west of Chester, and is the most northerly point to the England/Wales border other than the mud banks of the Dee estuary, and was therefore our only available walkable route once we were in Wales.

We drove down quite early considering it was the shortest journey to Wales, with the weather promising to be fair for the whole of the weekend.

The first stretch took us from the border to join a busier road before arriving at the Queensferry roundabout. Soon we were crossing over the girdered Queensferry bridge and into Queensferry itself, to follow what used to be the regular north Wales coast road before the days of the new A5 expressway.

Neither this section nor the next few miles had anything to write home about. We couldn't see the sea, the flat road was totally boring and very hard on the feet. We really stepped out on this part to get it over as quickly as we could, in fact, knowing what to expect, we'd often considered leaving this area out altogether but in the end we just felt it had to be done. Queensferry and the large steelworks at Shotton were most unattractive after some of the scenery of our earlier walks, and Connah's Quay seemed to be a main street of Indian and Chinese restaurants, betting shops and pubs. Flint, the county town, was a little better. This has been modernised and it was here we stopped to get plasters, cushioning and blister-stop as the fast pace was beginning to take it's toll on the old feet, particularly Dave's as he was only just breaking in a new pair of boots.

Eventually the industrialised area was left behind to an extent, and it was a little more pleasant as we approached Bagilt and then Mostyn, although with us still being on the main road, the sight, sound, and smell of the traffic was something we could have done without. Then just after Mostyn, we were able to leave the main road and take a minor one through the village of Ffynnongroew. As we were about to pass through the village we spotted a grass track and immediately took to it to have lunch.

It was approaching one o'clock by now, and we realised we had walked 18 miles this morning in about five hours, and that included a break plus a stop for shopping in Flint, that is an average of nearly 4 miles an hour—not bad that.

As we ate we could see that the track we were on led back onto the busy main road again, so once we were ready, having sorted out the feet, we headed in the direction of a footbridge that would get us across. Carrying on we followed the lane down to Talacre, the site of a Holiday Camp, then on through the campsite and round by the Point of Ayr colliery.

Then for the first time today, we enjoyed the luxury of walking on the soft sands of Talacre dunes. The tracks through the dunes were pretty well defined and we had no trouble in keeping a fairly straight path. Eventually the path led onto the beach but as we needed to veer inland to get to the town centre, we immediately found another track to take us through Prestatyn golf course. We followed this for half a mile or so past the clubhouse and onto the streets of Prestatyn. It was just a short walk to the railway station where we had arranged to meet up with the girls.

They had spent a nice day. After leaving us at Saughall early this morning, they had driven back to Chester and after morning coffee etc. they took the open-top bus for a guided tour of the city. Chester is a lovely place and after a walk round the shopping centre, a visit to the River Dee and lunch, they were ready to find us at Prestatyn.

For the second time, we stayed with Mrs. Hughes at Conway. It was lovely to be able to soak the feet after the pounding they'd taken today, before getting changed to go out in the evening. We went to the Austrian restaurant we had spotted on our last walk, but sadly they had no tables available so we ended up in the pub next door for a bar meal.

Day 22 Llandudno to Prestatyn 19 miles

The feet were still a bit sore after yesterday's effort, and we were aware there was a lot more hard road walking to come today, but we knew we just had to complete the link, otherwise it would mean another trip to north Wales.

After a good breakfast we drove out to the Little Orme to resume from our finishing point of last year. Leaving the girls, who were going to visit Bodnant Gardens today, we continued on the main road for about half a mile before the footpath led down to the sea front at Penrhyn. We stayed on this long promenade passing through Rhos-on-Sea and into Colwyn Bay. As we passed the place in Rhos where we had stopped for breakfast on the way to our very first walk nearly three and a half years ago, we reflected with some pleasure, and even some pride, of what had been achieved since then, realising at the same time that there was still a lot yet to be done.

At the far end of Colwyn beach, the promenade came to an abrupt end and we had to pass under the railway line and A55 to make the steep curling climb into Old Colwyn. Although we were quite high up, there was little to commend this route, and it was a bit frustrating to think that there was probably a coastal path somewhere down below, but finding a way to it was beyond us and we decided to stick to the road.

We carried on for another three miles gradually descending into Llanddulas where we had a stop for lunch. We sat on the grassy bank of the road by a roundabout, attracting many a glance from the passing motorists as we sat dusting our feet

with talcum powder with the contents of the
rucksacks scattered around socks, spare shirts,
yoghurt cartons, fruit and lunch-boxes.

Llanddulas beach was indicated as passing under
the A55, but we weren't too sure if there was a
continuous walk to Pensarn on the sands so we
played safe and stayed with the road route. As
we continued, we passed Gwrych Castle, a well
known landmark on the old coast road. It was
built in 1815, has 18 towers and is now a major
holiday attraction.

Soon we were able to cross the busy A55 by a
footbridge and a second one over the railway
line near to the caravan park. Then we were on
Abergele beach which we followed for a short
distance passing Pensarn and Towyn. Approaching
the Holiday Camp and caravan site at Kinmel Bay,
we were forced onto a walkway that led alongside
the railway line just on the other side of the sea
wall, noticeably strengthened after the severe
floods of a few years back. Walking through
the caravans, of which there were hundreds, we
could see that most of them were well boarded-up
against the elements. We crossed the bridge at
Rhyl and followed the promenade which was in the
process of being modernised, until a narrower
path ran alongside Rhyl golf course.

By now, Dave's feet were beginning to get painful
again and despite the good pace we can usually
manage, on this occasion we couldn't even keep
up with an old gent who must have been about
twenty years older than us.

The last three miles followed along the sea
front walkway and we ended the day at Prestatyn

Tourist Information Centre. The girls were there to meet us and it was time for home.

We had covered forty three miles this weekend and achieved our aim of completing the north Wales section, the one we had never really looked forward to, but had to be done. Now it is done, we've the happy prospect of the Pembrokeshire Coast Path, the Gower Peninsula and south Wales to look forward to—we can't wait.

CHAPTER TWELVE

June 1993

Day 23 St. Dogmaels to Newport
16 miles

The Pembrokeshire Coast Path at last. We'd heard about it, read about it and talked about it. Now it was here and we were ready to tackle it. The weather forecast was for good sunny weather all weekend which would be an added bonus.

We needed to be away from Stoke very early. Getting up to leave at 3.30 was no effort and in any case, an early start meant empty roads.

After picking up provisions in Cardigan, we got to St. Dogmaels, the start of the walk and were on our way. What a disappointing start though. It felt nothing like a coastal walk as we set off on the B4546 with cars streaming past including Norma and Jean who gave us a toot as they shot by. After we'd passed the Webley Hotel, there were good views of the sands and mudbanks of the Teifi estuary over on our right. We were now on a steady gradual climb. The main road veered left and our road became a country lane as we headed past Poppit Sands to eventually reach Allt-y-goed farm. Although we were three miles into the walk, it was only when we got to the farm that we saw the Pembrokeshire Coast Path signpost.

There was a grass footpath that led over the first of many stiles we would encounter and we started climbing steeply through the bracken heading for Caemes Head. Caemes Head is a nature reserve managed by the Dyfed Wildlife Trust. Near the top, the path turned sharply southwest and a wonderful view opened up. In the distance we could see the flashing light of Strumble Head lighthouse. Unfortunately, a heavy sea mist kept swirling in blocking out much of the magnificent scenery.

We were still climbing and soon came to the highest point on the whole of the national trail at 575 ft. The path often passed close to the edge of the cliffs, but at the most dangerous places short sections of fence had been erected to give some protection as well as written signs 'Cliffs can kill'.

There was a pretty cove to see at Pwllgranant and about a mile further on we reached Ceibwr Bay which is owned by the National Trust. Next came Pwlly Wrach, or the Witches Cauldron as it is known. This is classic marine erosion and the 'cauldron' itself is a collapsed cave formed where the sea has cut away at the softer sandstone and shale. The valleys which contain Ceibwr and Pwll y Wrach had steep gradients on both sides and it certainly made the old leg muscles pull somewhat.

The sea mist was quite annoying because it came in sporadically. At times we could hear the sound of a fog-horn out at sea. We later found out this was from the Customs and Excise launch which patrols this area of coast where drug smuggling has been known.

Past Caemes Head

High cliffs near Pwllgranant

View over Ceibwr Bay

A natural rock garden

Despite the glorious views being marred, we were still treated to the pleasure of lots of birds of which there are many colonies on the cliffs, and also what we called 'nature's rock garden'. There were several of these, just so natural and beautiful, made up of various tiny flowers, sea thrift, heathers, lichen and small ferns bedded on large boulders.

We followed the path walking for much of the time at more than 500 feet above sea level. Down below, there are a number of beaches used for breeding by Atlantic grey seals. Reaching Morfa Head was a bit of a milestone. From Dave's pedometer, maps and walking books, give or take a mile, we had completed 400 miles of our venture, about half way, so we celebrated with a Mars Bar and a carton of orange.

Near to Morfa Head

We started the gradual descent towards Newport passing the last of these wonderful 'gardens'.

Apparently each of these is a designated site of special scientific interest on the coastal footpath.

To reach Parrog boat club quay, the finishing point of today's walk, we could have stayed on the clifftop by the golf course or descend to the large beach of Traeth Mawr or Newport Sands. We chose the beach route now thick in sea mist, so dense that we couldn't see the sea. Arriving at the boathouse, we were lucky to find that it was low tide and we were able to cross the river by taking our boots off and wading, saving ourselves the longer alternative route via the bridge over the estuary.

The girls came to meet us and we found a cafe for a pot of tea. We were able to relax in the lovely sunshine as the mist was lifting quite quickly now. We talked of the day's events, then drove the short distance to our B&B in Newport.

This first section of the Pembrokeshire Coast Path is everything we had imagined, hard work admittedly, but very rewarding with such beautiful scenery. We were still talking about it as we ate a lovely meal in the evening at the Royal Oak in Newport.

Day 24 Newport to Fishguard 12 miles

The accommodation at Newport was quite good and we had an adequate breakfast to build us up for the day ahead.

After yesterday's super walk, we couldn't wait to get cracking in, once again beautiful fine weather.

We joined the path at the cafe where we had tea yesterday, passed in front of some cottages and headed west. Early on, the climbing was nothing like the stiff ascents of yesterday. We crossed sandy beaches at Aberrhigian and Aberfforest where families were enjoying themselves messing about on their boats in these idyllic little coves. We came across more of these during the day, some we crossed, others we viewed from the clifftop. This walking was certainly different from yesterday's rugged coastline.

The only signpost we saw for directions pointed inland through a copse although our guide-book indicated for us to turn right onto the exposed coast. We played safe by following the signposted route which was quite muddy after the recent rains, but it wasn't a big detour and we were soon in Soar Hill leading down to the beach at Cwm-yr-Eglwys or 'The Valley of the Church' and is one of Pembrokeshire's favourite beauty spots according to the literature. It certainly is a lovely area nestling at the eastern end of a great valley. The focal point is the ruined church of St. Brynach.

Now we were at Dinas Island and for the first time today we were in for a climb. In under a mile, from sea level we had reached the peak of the headland, Pen-y-Fan at 466 feet. We stopped for a while awaiting Jean and Norma who were coming up to the headland from the opposite direction.

We didn't have to wait too long. They'd made it and seemed pretty fresh as it was a stiff climb for them—well done girls. After a ten minute break taking photographs, the four of us walked down the path the girls had just taken. There was no mist today, just lovely sunshine, so we had tremendous views of the wonderful surrounding scenery as we headed for Pwllgwaelod.

There is a popular sandy beach at Pwllgwaelod and it also has a pub, cafe and restaurant. The girls had not had lunch, so no sooner had they said their cheerios, off they shot in search of food at the pub. For us it was a quite steep climb off the beach. When we stopped at the top of the cliffs a few minutes later, we turned back to wave but there was no sight of them—they'd obviously got their priorities right.

The four of us on the summit of Dinas Head

The cliffs weren't particularly high for the next few miles and the walking was very easy, but nevertheless it was still lovely countryside as the path wound through bracken and gorse. Above Hescwm, a well sheltered inlet, we stopped for lunch on the edge of a tilled field. It was so peaceful with just the sound of the many birds and the sea.

Overlooking Hescwm with Dinas Head in the background

Continuing we reached Penrhyn which still has traces of a First World War coastal defence installation. Now it has been developed into a caravan park, and from there we could make out the northern breakwater of Fishguard Harbour in the distance. Just before leaving the cliff path at Castle Point, we passed the ruins of Fishguard Fort, built in 1781 to defend the community against privateers. We joined the main road to take us through Fishguard 'Lower Town'.

The lower part of Fishguard has a totally different character from the modern town built on the hill above the Bay. Still recognisably an old fishing village set around wharves and quays, it made an ideal location for filming Dylan Thomas's 'Under Milk Wood' in the 1960s.

After crossing the old bridge, we climbed the hill—hard work in the hot weather—and followed the road until reaching 'The Slade', a small parklike walkway which kept to the shoreline and avoided walking through the town. Finally we arrived at Lampit Beach where Norma and Jean were sitting sunbathing in the gorgeous weather. They had spent most of the afternoon there after leaving us at lunchtime.

After enjoying half an hour relaxing ourselves, it was time for the long drive home, but we did break our journey at a roadside cafe near to Nevern. They sold traditional Welsh food and we had scones and two large pots of tea sitting outside at a picnic table beside a lovely wooded valley.

Climbing the hill out of Lower Fishguard

The cafe stop on the way home

This has been a brilliant weekend in which we've passed through the 400 mile mark, over half way now. The Coast Path itself has exceeded our wildest dreams by it's sheer beauty. There's still over 160 miles to go, and if it's anything like this first section, it will be heaven.

CHAPTER THIRTEEN

September 1993

Day 25 Fishguard to Abercastle
17 miles

For the first time, because of the long travel, we decided to have a four day break, Wednesday to Saturday, and pre-booked our B&B, a farmhouse at Croes-Goch. In fact we would look for farmhouse accommodation on all the walks from now on, one reason being that we stood a better chance of early breakfasts, which were necessary if we faced a long day's walking.

Again we had a lovely drive down to Fishguard. We had come to appreciate these journeys to and from the coast now that we were not using the A55, passing through some beautiful countryside, for example the stretch touching the Cambrian Mountains. We felt travelling was all part of the holiday, even if the girls tended to nod off from time to time.

The weather was very warm even early in the morning, and it was to turn out to be the warmest day of the year in Wales.

At 8.30am we were off leaving Lampit Beach along a lengthy, flat promenade before realising that we should have followed the road up the hill—all due to us prattling on instead of concentrating. Anyway we felt there would be a way off the promenade and eventually there was via a series of steps which joined the coast path north of Goodwick.

Jean and Norma in the meantime, relaxed at the beach awaiting the time to go off for their day out. In the Summer, Pembrokeshire has a free 'Coast Newspaper' for visitors which lists all sorts of activities organised under expert guidance, to suit all ages and interests. Activities include such things as beachcombing by torchlight, walking strenuous sections of the coast path, nature rambles, which was the girl's choice, and many more, but more of that later.

On the springy turf track, we made our way towards Carregwastad Point passing through Cwm Felin, a lovely wooded valley. Carregwastad Point is the scene of the last invasion of Britain in 1797 by the French, and a memorial stone has been erected at Carreg Goffa to commemorate the landing by an elderly Irish American called Colonel Tate and his invasion force of 1200 men. The badly prepared invaders, half of whom were prisoners released from jail on condition they joined the 'army', were attacked by a mixed force of Yeomanry and Fishguard villagers, many of them women, who accepted the Colonel's surrender.

On one of the stiles we climbed near to a lonely whitewashed cottage at Penrhyn, there was a sign which read "Beware Adders". Eventually we reached Strumble Head with it's white coastguard lookout building and the lighthouse clearly standing out. Quite a few people were at the headland as access is very easy by car. The path weaved in and out of little hillocks of volcanic rock now worn smooth, and there were tiny bays to pass en route, a particularly nice one being Porth Arian.

Gradually we were climbing arriving at the Youth Hostel at Pwll Deri, now walking at 450 ft. The hostel is totally exposed on the edge of the cliffs, but is in a spectacular position.

Penbwchdy with Strumble Head in the distance

Penbwchdy—the white building on the cliff is Pwll Deri Youth Hostel

The next few miles provided some absolutely magnificent scenery as we approached Penbwchdy, with huge masses of colour from the pink and maroon heather and the yellow gorse. It was quite breathtaking—'God's garden' we called it.

This colourful landscape continued for over a mile as we headed round the bay at Pwllcrochan and then made the gradual descent to Aber Mawr. The weather was very hot by now, so we took the opportunity to splash ourselves with water from the stream running onto Aber Mawr beach to cool down. We crossed the wide sandy beach, busy with holidaymakers, and rejoined the path.

Then it was just two and a half miles to the finish at the sheltered bay of Abercastle. This is a pretty little creek with a cluster of houses and cottages. There is also a lime kiln and the remains of a lime-burner's cottage. As Jean and Norma hadn't arrived, we called in the little craft shop and had some lemon tea from the vending machine, and it was really refreshing. Whilst we continued to wait, we were both beginning to stiffen up and, first me followed by Dave, both had an attack of cramp. We hopped around trying to ease it, and as Dave said, it would be known as the new sensational 'Cramp Dance'.

The girls eventually turned up and told us of their unusual day out at Nevern. After a few minutes getting changed, we were off up the steep hill to find the farmhouse at Croes-Goch. This looked fine and would suit us for the next three days.

Abercastle

We found a place to eat in the evening at the 'Square and Compass' pub, and after a good meal we were back at the farmhouse for a good night's sleep ready for tomorrow—after all we had been up since 3am.

Jean's account of "A day in the Countryside"

Walk—(10am—1pm) NEVERN—"Animal Tracks, Trails and Signs"—for all the family. 2 miles steady walking to identify the mammals found in woodlands. Wellingtons advisable.

So read the advert that attracted our eye. We had been pondering how to make the best use of our 'free time' while the menfolk were walking their coastline, and this activity as described in the Pembrokeshire Coast to Coast magazine appealed to us. Equipped with our jumpers, fleecy track-suit bottoms and wellingtons, as suggested, Norma and I waited for our guide to appear. He did, but not the one we expected. His name was Clive and, as a stand in, he didn't know the area, as he normally guided visitors around Skomer Island in his capacity as a bird and marine life expert. Anyway, several people arrived complete with young families similarly kitted the same as ourselves, so off we set.

It was very interesting. Nevern is historic, picturesque and beautifully kept. The church, very old, was full of interest as too was the churchyard with some very ancient yew trees and a magnificent Celtic Cross. Off then along the hedgerows to inspect various plants, insects, trees, birds etc.—the children and us too, had a wonderful time examining birds' nests, seed pods, animal signs and dens. However time was passing . . . . nearly two hours later.

By now, the weather was really beginning to warm up. We plodded on, along paths, down slopes, up hills and under trees, getting more than a little hungry and thirsty. People were taking it in turns to give the little ones a 'piggy back. We had hoped to go round full circle, but we were getting nowhere with no sign of a road either. We were lost! Poor Clive, he was an expert on marine and bird life but not the walks around Nevern. After a much needed rest sitting down on the edge of a field to let our feet cool down, as by now the sun was blazing down on us, we continued with a new heart. One hour later, we came to a tarmacked country lane and we literally ran along it until we reached a road—a main road, the A487. Traffic was whizzing past us—it was the Wednesday after the August Bank Holiday. We waited for the others, including Clive, and walked hopefully in the right direction on the grass verge. By now the heat was intense and we discovered later that it had turned out to be one of the hottest days of the year. We must have looked a funny sight—a group of people of all ages, some carrying little ones, dressed in warm trousers, some rolled up, jumpers tied around waists and nearly all wearing wellies. We had some funny looks from the occupants of passing vehicles! At last we came to a familiar landmark, the 'Pink Cafe' that straddled the road leading to Nevern village.

We raced towards it, almost ignoring the calls and goodbyes of the others. We paused and shouted back to them that we were going for a drink, a sit down and something to eat, and expressed our thanks for their company and cheerfulness, in the face of adversity . . . Staggering into the cafe, we flopped down. What a sight we must have looked—two middle-aged ladies, weary and red faced, dressed the way we were. As we sat waiting for our food and drink order, steam seemed to be rising as Norma and I had kicked off our wellies under the table.

The time was now 2.45 pm. four and three quarter hours after setting out, and certainly more than the two miles intended, had been covered on our woodland walk.

Then it was back to the car at Nevern church, and we drove down to meet up with Dave and Graham at Abercastle. We won't forget today in a hurry.

Day 26 Abercastle to St.Justinian's 16 miles

The accommodation at Trearched Farm was nice and comfortable, and we were given a good, substantial breakfast by Mrs. Jenkins, the owner. Over breakfast, we had a good laugh about the girl's day out yesterday. Today, they promised they wouldn't be taking the wellies, and unless they wanted to have a paddle in the sea without getting their feet wet, they shouldn't need to anyway, as the weather forecast was for a good sunny day again.

Trearched Farm at Croes-Goch

In perfect walking weather, we left Abercastle beach having been dropped off by the girls who were heading off to St. David's, At the pub last night, Dave had been talking to a bloke who had walked the route we would be taking today, warning him of a dangerous section early on. "I just closed my eyes and went for it" he said . . . . what a wimp! The only 'dangerous bit' we saw, was an unguarded part of the track a few feet in from the cliff edge, but it certainly wasn't any problem. In fact we spoke to a chap who was just packing his tent away, having been camped near the spot.

It was a nice steady climb, nothing strenuous, to Pen-Castell-coch which was a particularly beautiful area. Then we were heading down to Aber Draw which is the beach for Trefin. Trefin, just off the National Trail, is a busy little place and is the largest of the coastal villages between Goodwick and St. David's.

View from the farmhouse looking towards Trefin

The path climbed out of the valley and we noticed changes in the scenery as we were now in farmland and passed many ploughed fields running alongside the route.

We made our descent to Port Gain. This is a quaint place, and the harbour was used in the period 1837 to 1931 for the export of slate and bricks. It still has the remains of the old brickworks and the huge bins that held the crushed stone. We continued at a fairly good pace as the path was reasonably on the level.

Eventually we swung southwards passing above Traeth Llyfn before arriving at Abereiddi Bay. The sand on this beach is black, caused by fine particles of slate pounded by the sea over centuries. From Abereiddi, after a short stretch on the road, we were climbing very gradually at first, but just past Porth-y-Rhaw the path suddenly climbed very steeply as we skirted the huge mound, Carn Penberry. It made the old legs ache a bit. This solitary climb was temporary however, and soon we had dropped down to face a much easier stretch, but before carrying on, we stopped for lunch in splendid, colourful scenery and could have sat for much longer than the forty five minutes we allow ourselves for all lunch breaks now.

West of Penberry, most of the coast is in the ownership of the National Trust, and after Penllechwen peninsula as we headed towards St. David's Head in the distance, several paths running parallel to each other opened up and we could have taken any of them as all were leading to the same end point. We made our choice of route and followed it through more masses of wild flowers and ferns.

Eventually we reached St. David's Head and could afford the luxury of a short break as we were well ahead of schedule. A coach party of Americans on a tour of the West Country and Wales, had strolled out to the headland from Whitesands Bay. We chatted to a couple of husbands and wives who weren't too impressed with the coach driver who had said they needn't take any walking shoes etc. and here they were in open-toed sandals and plastic macs scrambling over rocks. "The guy's a jerk" they said.

St. David's Head

Continuing, we crossed the stream by the tiny beach of Porthmeglan and less than half a mile later, we were on Porth Mawr or Whitesands Bay. This is a glorious stretch of sand and holds the 'blue flag' of high esteem. It is voted the cleanest beach in Wales and not surprising too.

Soon we were passing above the last beach on this section, Porthselau, and after this it was a nice easy stretch to finish the day at St. Justinian's. Just before the finish, we met a lady walking in the opposite direction. We stopped for a chat and she was very interested in our Welsh venture. Having said our goodbyes, we walked to the lifeboat station, little thinking that we would meet her again—but more of that later.

At the lifeboat station, the BBC were filming "Lifeboat", a TV drama series and had just packed up for the day when the girls arrived. They told us of their day at St. David's, enjoying a visit to the sea zoo and then going on to an unusual garden. The owner had gathered and assembled a collection of rare and unique plants from all over the world.

St. Justinian's lifeboat station looking towards Ramsey Island

Then it was back to the farmhouse for a refreshing shower and change before going out for something to eat. We drove out to Letterston where there is an award winning fish and chip restaurant and takeaway called 'Something's Cooking'. Unfortunately Dave was having some discomfort from a couple of nasty blisters. He'd have to give them some treatment before bed so as to be fit for tomorrow.

Day 27 St. Justinian to Newgale
17 miles

Dave's feet had not recovered enough to be tackling a long walk so we took the day off, resting and sightseeing, something we're not used to. Norma and Jean left us in St. David's to do some shopping after the four of us had visited the Cathedral. We explored the town and, in doing so, bumped into the lady we had met the day before. Her name was Thelma and she came from the London area. She owned a cottage at Port Clais and asked if we would be interested in renting it on our trips to west Wales. We told her that we would get the girls to meet her at the cottage tomorrow to look it over, and we'd try to arrange to be walking Port Clais around the same time and maybe call ourselves.

More importantly to us though, she recommended a particular brand of blister treatment kit, obtainable from the local chemist and this was to prove invaluable advice. The afternoon was spent wandering round the shops in Haverfordwest, but Dave and I weren't too enthusiastic—walking not shopping is the thing we do best.

Back to today's walk . . . .

Again it was perfect walking weather as we left the lifeboat station. Dave had applied the blister plasters and he felt pretty good. The early stages were very easy. We had good views of Ramsey Island as at one point, we were only about half a mile off it's shoreline. The path continued along Ramsey Sound until reaching Pen Dal-aderyn, the most westerly point of the whole Coast Path, and soon we were swinging eastwards making a gradual climb, but certainly not stiff. Then we were back into National Trust land as we passed Porthlysgi, and a mile further on, we dropped down to Port Clais.

Porth Clais is the harbour for the city of St. David's, used by saints, disciples and pilgrims during the 'Age of the Saints', and by little trading vessels during the centuries that followed.

Here we had arranged to meet the girls and were a little delayed waiting for them. They had met Thelma, and although the cottage was nice, it was a little pricey, and in any case, on these walking holidays, we didn't want to be cooking meals etc . . . Perhaps it would do for a family break some other time.

We continued. Still heading eastwards, we passed St. Non's Bay and the popular Caerffi Bay. St. Non's Bay is a place of peace, named after the mother of St. David. There were some ascents and descents around these bays, and at the next, Porth y Rhaw, there was a very steep gradient on both sides of the valley. A mile later, we were at Solva.

Solva

Solva is an absolutely delightful village, and the first sight of the creek way below us as we came round the headland, gave a marvellous spectacle. We made our way down to the harbour by passing through Upper Solva and crossing the little bridge by the pub which was doing great business in the lovely warm weather. We were tempted to have a pint ourselves, but thought better of it and settled for our usual cardboard carton fruit drink with our lunch, eaten at one of the benches at the water's edge. We felt so relaxed in such wonderful surroundings.

Dave's feet had survived the morning session well, and before resuming, here was a good opportunity to replace the 'blister plaster'. Good old Thelma.

On the way again, the path climbed immediately, quite steeply to the Gribin Ridge, descended just as steeply down into the Gwadn, across the valley then re-ascended to the clifftop. In fact, there was a lot of switchback on this stretch of the path.

Clifftop path beyond Upper Solva which can be seen on the right

Whilst on this stretch, we met a man out walking with his young daughter. He was Welsh and showed interest when we told him of our venture to walk the whole coastline of Wales and not just the Pembrokeshire Coast Path. He said he lived in Swansea, and when we would be doing that section, we would walk right past his door. The scenery on the Gower peninsula was even better than Pembrokeshire, he felt, although from what we have experienced so far, this would take some believing—we'll have to see.

At Porthmynawyd there was a cute little valley with the path twisting and winding through ferns, brambles and willows. The path then suddenly dropped and we were on the north-eastern corner of St. Bride's Bay which was to lead us onto Newgale beach. This beach is about two and a half miles long, and having walked roughly a mile along the sand and pebbles, we reached the carpark and the end of today's walk.

Approaching Newgale

Having met Jean and Norma on the car-park, it was heaven after the warm day, to enjoy an ice-cream before we packed all the gear away to return home. We had been so impressed with Solva that we took the girls back there to show them. We stayed about twenty minutes just strolling around—they were just as impressed themselves.

Then it was time to go, but we ended our stay in Wales for the time being, with fish and chips on the quayside at Fishguard, agreeing that this had been yet again, another enjoyable break, especially with such good weather.

CHAPTER FOURTEEN

October 1993

Day 28 Chepstow to Nash 18 miles

Autumn is here now and as we'd agreed earlier, the walks would have to be in areas easy to get to because of the travelling and shorter days.

We used yet another route in getting to Wales, this time down the M6,M5 and M4 across the Severn Bridge to Chepstow. It was typical back-end weather, cool with a ground frost, but at least we were in sunshine.

When we planned our venture originally, we were going to finish it with the final strides into Chepstow on the English / Welsh border, but we've been so smitten with coastal walking, particularly Pembrokeshire, that it wouldn't be fitting to end a coastline walk in a town, so we've altered our plan and will have to decide on another finishing point. It will certainly be on a coastal stretch, maybe somewhere in the south Wales area.

Today's walk started just past a roundabout over the Severn Bridge, and already we were glad we'd changed our plan—imagine finishing a 750 odd mile walk at an insignificant roundabout. There are walks apparently down by the Severn estuary, but as we didn't have a Pathfinder map for this area, and didn't want to run the risk of having to constantly backtrack if trails became confusing, we decided to stick with roads and country lanes running parallel to the estuary.

Having crossed a field, we joined the golf course at Mathern, and having wandered around the playing area, leaving great footprints in the frost-laden grass, we found a public footpath to take us past the clubhouse and onto a main road for a short way, then a secondary one to lead us through the small village of Portskewett. Just a mile further on, we were at the little market town of Caldicot. The girls had spent a couple of hours in the town visiting the castle and the inevitable tearoom.

Carrying on, on what was beginning to be a most uninspiring walk, we eventually left the major road at Undy and followed country lanes until it was time to stop for lunch. Whilst eating, we got a little confused as to exactly where we were. Now we were paying the price of not having a decent map for the area as we just could not get our bearings. Obviously, as with Dwyran back on Anglesey, a new road had been built which didn't show on our old road atlas. We had to stop a local out walking and ask for directions and he put us right. Soon we were back on our intended route via a series of more country lanes.

At Goldcliff, a couple of lady horse riders who were out gathering names for a petition, stopped to talk to us. They were telling us of the proposed new by-pass in Newport, and the resentment felt by the locals. In fact they suggested that even though we were only just visitors to the area, we could still sign the petition.

As we left Goldcliff, we had the sight and smell of the Llanwern steel works in the distance as we headed towards Nash.

Steel Works at Llanwern

At Nash we were in for a couple of surprises. First, as we were passing one of the houses in the village, we heard a shout and a man came running out. He said that earlier on, heading home from Newport, he had seen two ladies—Jean and Norma—wandering around appearing to be lost. He asked if he could help. They were looking for the bridge to get across the River Usk where we had arranged to meet. What we hadn't realised was that the bridge we'd indicated was a transporter bridge which carries cars on a moving platform across the river, and not the footbridge in the town itself. He explained to the girls it would mean about an hour's walk to reach the far side, so he told them to wait and he would look out for us, hence the shout.

He took us in his car to where the girls were waiting and we thanked him for his help and the lift. Unfortunately for Dave and I, it would mean a return to Nash to walk the stretch into Newport, otherwise we would have missed out a section—and we couldn't have that. To keep on schedule for the weekend though, we would fit in the unwalked bit some other time. Then came the second surprise.

On enquiring into B&B accommodation in Newport, the Tourist Information Office had recommended the old converted West Usk lighthouse, a few miles down the road at St. Bride's Wentlooge. We had some problems finding it, but when we did, it was really fantastic. It was most unusual, but beautifully furnished, well laid out and very comfortable. The owner, a Londoner, and his French wife, were still in the process of planning further work on the roof section to convert it into a terraced area with a bar in the lamp-room. They were both keen environmentalists and actively involved in the by-pass protest. In the reception area, they even had an authentic original 'Dalek' from the BBC series, 'Doctor Who', and they intended getting maximum publicity by using it in the campaign.

Our unusual B&B at West Usk lighthouse

Dave and Norma's bedroom

A second bedroom   Jean and Norma on the roof

In the evening, we went out for a meal at the local restaurant where they served a huge paella which Jean and I had, but couldn't finish, while Dave and Norma settled for the more modest steak and kidney pie. Then it was back for our first ever sleep in a lighthouse.

Day 29 West Usk lighthouse to Lavernock Point 16 miles

Lighthouse or not, we all had a good night's sleep in our unusual surroundings and polished off a good full breakfast next morning.

Through the gate and it's nine miles to Cardiff

Staying in the lighthouse had provided us with a bonus as regards to the walk. The owner told us the path outside through the gate would take us virtually all the way into Cardiff. Had we not known of this, we would made our way back to the main road and battled with the traffic.

The path in fact, is a low rampart which has protected the low level hamlets and villages along the road to Cardiff from the sea for centuries. In 1606, the water rose 6 feet above ground level causing great damage. The flat meadows around about are criss-crossed with an elaborate network of drainage ditches and channels to carry rainwater through sluice gates to the sea.

It was such an easy track to walk on, flat as a pancake with no interruptions. On a lovely Autumn morning, many were taking advantage of the weather. There was lots of activity. Fishermen on the shore side were obviously engaged in some angling competition, while further along on the land side, the local golf course was in full swing. In the distance, beyond the golfers, we could see the road we had originally planned on walking, now getting quite busy.

We continued on this coastal track until eventually we were forced to take to the road where a sign read 'Welcome to Cardiff'. For the capital of Wales though, it did seem very quiet even for a Sunday morning, and as we made our way through the pedestrianised shopping area, we could very nearly count on one hand the number of people we saw.

Soon we came to the Castle with Jean and Norma there as arranged. They'd enjoyed themselves that morning touring the castle itself. We all had lunch together in the car, before driving down to the docks area to resume the route we would have been on had we not diverted to meet meet the girls.

Norma dropped us off, and we continued to Penarth Road, which was to take us past the Marina and give us the opportunity to get down onto the beach, rocky at first, but then leading onto a better sandy stretch. At the pier, we left the beach, and actually took a little stroll on the pier before having a stop for an ice cream on Penarth promenade which was very busy now.

The promenade eventually turned inland, but we found a narrow shrub lined walkway that took us onto the cliffs above the beach, and ended in a lane at Lavernock Point. At the church, where we met up with the girls once more, there was a plaque on the wall, erected to commemorate the first radio message sent from Lavernock to Brean Down across the Severn by Marconi in 1879. That was something we didn't know, so this stage of the walk has been educational if nothing else.

So that was it for this year, and as we drove home, we were already planning 1994—the Gower Peninsula and more Pembrokeshire. We can't wait.

CHAPTER FIFTEEN

April 1994

Day 30 Nash to West Usk lighthouse
8 miles

Port Talbot to Swansea 11 miles

It was Easter Sunday, and we were up very early and on the road by 4.30am. The first stage of the walk today was to complete the section we had missed out last October.

The weather was coolish, and although winter was at an end, there was snow on the Black Mountains and Brecon Beacons in the far distance as we drove through Ross-on-Wye and Monmouth.

We were soon changed ready for action and walking by 8am. having arranged to meet Norma and Jean at the lighthouse. It was just country lane walking as we passed through Pye Corner and soon we were on the outskirts of Newport, deserted so early in the morning. Newport isn't a particularly inspiring place walkwise, especially as the route took us round the docks area passing the Transporter Bridge, bringing back memories of our last walk.

The Transporter Bridge is a landmark of Newport which can be seen for miles around. It was built in 1906, and it's unusual design was made necessary by the low river banks and the need to clear the tall masts of ships. An arched bridge would have been too steep and more expensive to build. It is possible to climb the stairs to the towers and walk across the river on the upper deck enjoying spectacular views of the city, 240 feet above the river, but frankly, you would have to be a nutcase to do it, as it is basically an open, girdered construction. Certainly, it wasn't for Dave or I.

The docks area was very tatty, as I suppose most dock areas are. There were many boarded up properties, one we noticed had a window blocked horizontally with a door. Things got a little better as we progressed on the road to take us on the outskirts of the town, and soon we were clear of the industrialised area and into the lane that led to the lighthouse. About half a mile from the finish, we felt the first drops of rain, and with the girls already there to meet us, there was no hanging about and we were quickly back to Newport to pick up the M4 motorway to take us onto Port Talbot, coming off at Junction 40.

The rain was continuous by now and as we sat in the car at Port Talbot having lunch, we spilled a packet of powdered milk, brushed it into the road and immediately formed a white river in the gutter. We were beginning to question whether or not to carry on in this miserable weather, but having come so far, and taking into consideration that if we didn't continue, we wouldn't finish the Gower on this visit to Wales, we decided to hope for the best and walk.

The walk itself was all on the roads. Though we had noticed that there may have been a chance to walk on the towpath of the Neath Canal, we decided not to risk it. The road ran very close to the motorway, and so as to avoid close contact continually, we took a side road which in actual fact took us further away from our route and we found we were heading towards Neath. Realising the mistake, we doubled back and found the road that led over the bridge at Briton Ferry.

The final five miles into Swansea were none too exciting, firstly because the scenery on the coast side was spoiled by lots of huge storage tanks in this heavily industrialised area, and secondly, the rain, which had been on and off, now began to get heavier and we were getting a right good soaking, but it didn't stop us having a good laugh. We didn't see anyone else out walking, after all, anyone with sense would be indoors, and who could blame them.

We met the girls at Swansea Leisure Centre and found our way to Knelston. This wasn't easy, as we missed the road a couple of times, and even struggled to find our B&B accomodation once we were in Knelston, and it's only a tiny village. At one point, we drove up a muddy cart track, convinced we were right, only to find it wasn't, and poor old Norma had to reverse for a couple of hundred yards with a water filled ditch on both sides, as we couldn't turn round.

Eventually we made it, and once showered and changed into dry clothes, we soon forgot all about the weather and looked forward to the next three day's holiday at our latest accomodation, and what a 'find' this turned out to be, especially as we could get an evening meal in. We finished the day with a dinner of the very highest standard.

Day 31 Oxwich Bay to Swansea 18 miles

The walking gear had dried out well, and thankfully the rain had disappeared although there was a fairly cool wind and just a little sun as we set off.

We made our way past Oxwich village to arrive on the 2 mile stretch of beach, and headed towards Three Cliffs Bay at the far end. The cliffs in the area have suffered from erosion over the ages, with one impressive effect being the natural arch through the three crags that gives the bay it's name.

After leaving the beach, we scrambled up into fields, didn't concentrate on our coastal route, and ended up crossing more fields and onto a busy road, totally missing out Pwlldu Head and Brandy Cove. As we didn't fancy retracing our steps, we decided to carry on along the road, although from time to time we were able to get onto a woodland track that ran parallel, but we never lost the sight and sound of the traffic.

Eventually a minor road opened up to the right and we followed this for about a mile when we were able to pick up a foot path taking us back towards the coast. Then came a pleasant wooded section where we decided to stop for lunch.

Just as we were about to resume after, we met a young lady out walking. We had a nice chat and it turned out she was from the nearby village of Pyle. As we were all going in the same direction, we walked together for about a mile or so. She called us 'professional walkers', but we couldn't agree less. Anyway, her local knowledge was of great benefit and she was able to point us in the direction of the coast path which would lead us to the Mumbles. Without her help we could have wasted an awful lot of time trying to get down tracks to beaches only to find they would lead to nowhere. When we reached her village, we thanked her, said our goodbyes and carried on. We did miss one path from a small beach and ended up back on the road via a rough farm track, but after a couple of hundred yards we were back into a field to pick up the clifftop path once again. Apart from the short tree-lined stretch into Newton at Langland Bay, we were able to stay on the cliffs all the way to the Mumbles.

Mumbles Head and Lighthouse

Mumbles Head was extremely busy today with it being Easter Monday and we had to thread our way through the crowds to carry on along Mumbles Road. We were now down on flat promenade with easy walking for the last four miles, the route being shared with a 'cycle way' virtually all the way into Swansea. We skirted the marina and made our way to our pre-arranged meeting place with the girls who were late today. They had been to visit the nearby town of Brecon. Swansea was looking much nicer today after yesterday's washout.

Soon Norma and Jean arrived and we were soon travelling back to Knelston. Mrs Williams had prepared yet another excellent evening meal. Everything about this accommodation was perfect, beautifully decorated, modern designer furniture and brilliant food to go with it. We were all very impressed.

Day 32 Llanmadoc to Oxwich Bay
16 miles

Again the weather was dry and sunny but very breezy as we set off. We geared up by the pub at Llanmadoc and climbed the hill on a minor road before turning into a country lane. At the end of the lane we came to a gate leading to the sea at Broughton Bay. Through the gate we followed a track that headed left through a little copse and onto the outskirts of a pleasantly situated caravan site. Finally we reached the sand dunes of Whitland Burrows. Walking in the very soft sand made progress slow, but steadily we made our way towards the sea and the large expanse of beach at Rhossili Bay.

In the dunes at Whitland Burrows

The coast path above Rhossili beach

Rhossili was very impressive as the wind was whipping the sea into a mass of white foam.

At one point, we felt we would make better progress by leaving the beach and getting onto the firmer track running along the cliff top. This involved scaling a very steep face of dry, soft sand which was extremely difficult. With nothing to hang on to, it seemed like it was one step up and two down. It took about ten minutes to move forward ten yards. So much for our 'better progress'.

Once on the coast path, it was easy walking right along to Worm's Head. This is a very popular spot for visitors. It has a cafe, and an observation point. After we had cleared this section, we made it back to the cliff path where we ate our lunch seated in the bushes to shelter from the strong breeze.

With it being such a clear day, we had tremendous views over Swansea Bay as we resumed the trail, and this was a particularly pleasant stretch. Eventually the path began to descend as we approached Port Eynon Bay. The footpath got a little confusing in a mass of sand dunes above a small beach, and we ended up crossing a field to get to the beach area of Port Eynon. Being Bank Holiday week, there were plenty of people about, although most were well wrapped up against the cool weather. After a short stop we returned to the path and it was very easy walking on a flat grass track, just a bit muddy after the weekend rain. We felt we were well on time and had no wish to hurry the last four and a half miles. However, problems lay ahead!

As we came round the final headland towards Oxwich, we entered a nature reserve. Although we thought there would be easy access to Oxwich beach, the path began to climb very steeply into a wooded area and continued climbing for quite some way, in fact we counted a hundred steps up. The beach we wanted was now becoming a dot way below, and with this extra walking we were beginning to feel that we would be late back for our evening meal.

At long last the track levelled out. It was all of a hundred and fifty yards long before descending another hundred steps down. Anyone who thinks going downhill is easy couldn't be further from the truth—take our word for it. It certainly wasn't easy on this section as the churned up path was extremely slippery and great care had to be taken, otherwise we could have ended up in thick and prickly undergrowth. We were getting quite ratty by now and we could well have done without this last inconvenient stretch.

By now we had arrived on the final section, and all our frustrations and what we thought of whoever designed the Oxwich Bay Nature Reserve footpath, were in the past and we realised that we could just about make it back in time for our meal, even if it meant having to shower later. A few more yards and we made it back to the waiting girls on the car park at Oxwich, and within ten minutes we were back at Knelston. It was still a bit hectic though, having only about a quarter of an hour to get ready for dinner and our last night on the Gower peninsula.

Day 33 Llanmadoc to Loughor 12 miles

Today it was time to say goodbye to the Gower Peninsula, and weatherwise it was probably the best day of our break, sunny but not too warm, and the strong wind of yesterday had dropped to just a breeze. As we packed to leave, one thing we all agreed on was that the B&B accommodation at Mrs William's bungalow had been absolutely first class.

We returned to the pub car park at Llanmadoc and this time headed off towards Cheriton on a country lane. This led into the tiny village and there we saw a public footpath signpost directing us into a field that was supposedly to take us onto a track by the marshes of Llanrhidian Sands. As usual, with farmland type paths there was some difficulty negotiating our way, and after having spent considerable time in very boggy conditions, we took the first opportunity to get back onto the road by climbing over a barb-wired fence. We were probably trespassing but who cares? They should make the signs a little clearer. Eventually we were back on the road again just before Weobley Castle at Landimore. The castle was built in the early 14th century, but from the late 15th century, the building became a fortified manor house. As we passed, we could see lots of cars down the long drive, and it seemed some form of archery get-together was taking place.

This road continued for a couple of miles and eventually headed us in the direction of the marshes but this time we walked on a decent concreted path by the reeds. Obviously this had been constructed to give access to birdwatchers and we passed one or two land-rovers as we carried on. At the end of the road we came to the pleasant village of Crofty, and having just passed through it, we parked ourselves down on a grassy bank for a spot of lunch.

The afternoon section was all on roadway, although we did try to find a track by the mud flats but soon gave up. When I say 'on the road', it literally was for Dave who tripped over the kerb and went a right purler, grazing his knees and elbows in the process. He's a brave lad though, dusted himself down and just carried on. I gave him a 5.8 out of 6 for the artistic impression.

Eventually we reached Gowerton and cut through a small copse before joining the lane to take us into Loughor—pronounced 'Lacker'. This was quite a busy little place having lots of shops and also has a Castle ruins.

As Jean and Norma had not arrived, we found there was time to walk across the long bridge and back spanning the River Burry, to take us to the outskirts of Llanelli, a good starting point for a future walk.

After meeting up and having a quick bite and drink, it was time to return home, this time trying yet another route through Merthyr Tydfil and Abergavenny which gave some magnificent scenery.

We've enjoyed our four day break very much, despite the wet start but we have to disagree with our walker friend who we met at Solva, last September. Although there are certainly many beautiful areas on the Gower Peninsula, from our experience, it comes second to the Pembrokeshire Coast Path.

One final note to end on—we have now passed through the five hundred mile mark.

CHAPTER SIXTEEN

June 1994

Day 34 Musselwick to Sandy Haven
19 miles

For the third time we returned to Pembrokeshire and once again we had glorious weather to go with it. We really have been so lucky on our walks in this part of Wales to have picked such good weather each time.

On this walking break, we found we needed to use our heads as well as our feet, because we had to negotiate two tidal creek crossings—one at the River Gann and the other at Sandy Haven. At the Gann there is about a four hour period around low-water in which to cross, and the same timings apply at Sandy Haven. As it takes roughly two hours to walk between the two, it was essential to be leaving Pickleridge—that is the sandy stretch of beach between Dale and the Gann, on a falling tide. If we got the timings wrong, it would mean taking the 'high water detour' and we would have to walk three times as far to reach the eastern side of Sandy Haven creek.

We had enquired in advance for the tide-tables on the days we would be walking, so that we could calculate a lunch stop to coincide with the falling tide, and decided that setting out from Musselwick Sands near the village of Marloes, would not only be the most suitable for the crossing, it would also give us a comfortable day's walking from Musselwick to Newgale on the final day and thus complete the link.

Just before leaving Marloe's Beacon where we had parked the car to get kitted up, whilst arranging a meeting place at Sandy Haven with the girls, a man out walking his dog overheard us and commented that he had walked this area many times and thought we might be a bit ambitious to meet our schedule, but we had no doubts and gave it no second thought. After all, he doesn't know how experienced we have become by now.

There was a track to take us from the lane across a field to join the coast path at Black Cliff above Musselwick Sands. Less than two miles later and we were walking through Martin's Haven, the departure point for the Skomer Island boats. There were quite a few people milling about here, so presumably there was a sailing due.

The path now entered the Deer Park, a headland of some six and a half miles in length, and from here we had good views of Skomer Island with Skokholm further in the distance.

Next came the long stretch of beach at Marloe's Sands, although we decided to stay on the clifftop and away from the soft looking sand. There was easy walking above Red Cliff and Hooper's Point, and soon we reached Westdale Bay which starts the Dale peninsula. From Westdale looking inland, we could see Dale Castle less than half a mile away quite clearly, and Dale village further in the distance. In fact, the neck of the peninsula at this point is less than a mile across, but our route on the coast path would take us over five miles further, but who cares when walking in wonderful scenery like this. We reached the Coastguard HQ at St. Ann's Head and passed in front of a row of ex Trinity House cottages before continuing above Mill Bay. There were lush wooded valleys to cross at Watwick and Castlebeach bays as we headed towards Dale.

Mill Bay is where in August 1485, Henry Tudor landed with 2000 men. From Here he marched through Wales and 15 days after his landing, he and his allies won the famous battle for the English crown at Bosworth Field.

Dale beach

Dale is an old trading and fishing port. Fishing, shipbuilding and general trading were the main activities. Now there are only three fishing boats in the village, and Dale has become a popular

watersports centre. It was busy today with lots
of activity on the sea—yachting, windsurfing and
boating. This was where we had planned our lunch
stop prior to the tidal crossing, and we'd got
it just perfect. Even as we ate, the tide was
ebbing quickly and by the time we were ready to
resume, there were large areas of exposed sand,
leaving us no problem with the crossing.

However in our excitement at having got it right,
we missed the coast path sign, came off the beach
too early and ended up straying into someone's
back garden. We felt a bit guilty about this,
but by creeping down the side of the house, we
recovered our position and found our way back
onto the proper trail.

Continuing, we passed through a lovely wooded
valley to reach Monk's Haven and then had an
easy section along the sandstone cliffs passing
Watch House Bay and Lindsway Bay. This is chiefly
notable as the place where HRH The Prince of
Wales first set foot on Welsh soil in 1955.

After passing Great Castle Head, we were at
Sandy Haven, a lovely spot with Sandyhaven Pill
emptied and filled with every tidal cycle. We'd
got our timing perfect and had plenty of time to
spare to cross over the short stretch of beach
on the stepping stones with the sea still well
out. So much for the man we'd met back at Marloes
this morning, doubting our ability to meet our
schedule. We know what we're doing.

Norma came to meet us in the car, and as she was
facing the wrong way, we walked back down the
lane from the creek to show her a turning point.
Once she'd turned, she shot off up the hill not

waiting for us—the old meanie. It meant we'd walked up the hill twice, and it was a couple of hundred yards further before we found them on a caravan park.

Soon we were on our way to St. Petrox and our accommodation at Bangeston Farm.

Day 35 Pembroke to Freshwater West 18 miles

It was a lovely farmhouse at St. Petrox, and Mrs Matthias had cooked us an appetising meal last night, so after a good, typical farmhouse breakfast, we were off to Pembroke town to continue our walking in beautiful weather yet again.

Starting in the main street, we had just a short section through the streets round by the castle before heading towards Monkton, leaving the road and first dropping into a valley to be followed by a lane uphill. Now for the first time in Pembrokeshire, we were seeing the industrialised section of the coast path as the 750 ft chimney stack of Pembroke power station came into view.

We got a little confused on the track just after entering the fields as there was a single strand of wire dividing the marked route. Undecided as to which to take, we headed off up the hill, which, as it turned out was the wrong choice, and walked through the village of Hundleton before rejoining the correct path half a mile further on. We passed through a little wet, wooded section as we made our way towards the

Pembroke River estuary, passing very close to the power station. At Pwllcrochan we entered a lane which took us past the church. This lane continued for about three quarters of a mile and then reverted to a track taking us below the pier jetty of the Texaco refinery with it's five berths, the longest of which can handle 300,000 ton supertankers.

Soon we were at Bulwell Bay which is only a few yards long, then climbed up through scrub and bracken cutting slightly inland. We passed the redundant jetty once used for the import of crude oil to the BP Ocean Terminal before joining an asphalt road past the old oil tank site. Over on our right was Fort Popton, another of the Victorian defences of the waterway, built around 1860. After the closure of the BP Ocean Terminal the building was empty for some years, but it now houses a Field Studies Council Research Centre.

We followed this easy flat road at water level and then descended to the shore of Angle Bay to take us to Angle village. This shoreline was very stony and not too easy on the feet, but eventually we were able to climb onto a walled footpath which led to the little creek at Angle. We took a short cut through the creek against the advice of the guide-book which entailed us tangling with a lot of mud. Still, it was lunchtime now and the mud-caked boots soon dried as we sat eating at the water's edge.

We continued after lunch climbing past the busy pub, then rounded Angle Point and passed above the old lifeboat station now in a derelict condition. The modern lifeboat station is opposite the redundant Esso jetty, well sheltered from the south-westerlies. The climb was very steady and it was easy walking as we rounded the headland to descend to West Angle Bay. In the lovely weather, this beach was quite busy. Just offshore was Thorn Island. The island fort, built in the 1850s, is still in a good state of repair and is now a hotel. It was amazing that in just a matter of a mile or so, we had lost sight of the oil refineries were back in the world of super scenery.

Out of West Angle Bay, we climbed the wide grassy bank and headed west passing the disused RAF radio station. The site and it's modern building is now used by university radar research which investigates offshore wave characteristics—very technical. The path in this stretch was marked with stakes which walkers are ordered to walk within, but soon we were on the familiar track lined with bracken and gorse, with more magnificent views down the coastline. We could see the Castlemartin peninsula quite clearly in the far distance as we headed on. As we walked southeastwards, we could see traces of Angle airfield built in the winter of 1940-41.

Just past Angle   Approaching Freshwater
                              West

There was quite a bit of switchback on this
stretch, but none of the climbs or descents were
at all difficult and we were making good time.
Eventually the path began to drop quite steeply
around East Pickard Bay. At many of the stiles
we have crossed up to now, there have been many
warnings posted about the dangers on the cliffs,
and yet here, which we considered to be very
dangerous, no sign was in evidence. The danger
lay in the fact that the path cut through an open,
smooth grassy field which sloped down to the
cliff edge about 50 yards away, with nothing to
stop anyone slipping in wet conditions. Anyway,
today was extremely dry and no care was needed.

Freshwater West is about 2.5 miles long and after
descending to the beach, we walked alongside the
edge of a calm sea to the far end of the beach
where the girls were waiting. They're really
brilliant at finding the pick up point at the
end of a day's walking, especially as many of
the meeting places none of us have seen before.

Then it was back to Bangeston Farm for showers,
change, a lovely meal and a drive out through
Angle seeing the Texaco refinery lit up in the
dark—fantastic!

Day 36 Pembroke to Sandy Haven
16 miles

It was time to link the two unwalked sections of
the Coast Path, and this time we didn't have to
worry about the tide at Sandy Haven as our walk
would finish on the near side of the bay.

We said our goodbyes to Mrs Matthias promising to be back next year for the completion of Pembrokeshire, and headed into Pembroke town. After getting geared up we set off and immediately crossed over the river and veered off to the right into a series of farm fields, all with rights of way. Eventually the track took a sharp right and we continued up the grassy slope through woodland to emerge into the backstreets of Pembroke Dock.

There was a good two mile stretch through the streets busy with shoppers. We passed the massive defensive wall of the Royal Naval Dockyard and the disused Martello tower, built around 1850. Now at last, we were clear of the town and climbed the hill to the Cleddau Bridge.

View from Cleddau Bridge

We crossed the lengthy bridge which gave great views above the river estuary and beyond. In the far distance we could see Angle Point looking quite different today surrounded by a skyline of chimneys and tanks of the power station and refineries.

Soon we reached Neyland and dropped down under the bridge to pass the Yacht Club with a very popular marina judging by the number of boats we saw. Neyland, a planned town, owes it's origin to Isambard Kingdom Brunel who made it the terminus for his South Wales Railway in 1856, but it disappeared in 1955 following Lord Beeching's axing of the railways. However, after a period of decline, Neyland is now thriving with factory units and housing development springing up.

For the next two miles, it was easy walking at sea level passing the church at Llanstadwell before the trail began to climb from Hazelbeach to bring us into close contact with the Gulf refinery. To cross the jetty approach road. we walked through an iron caged footbridge followed by a second over the pipeline connecting jetty and refinery.

Crossing the pipelines through the iron cage

137

These enclosed walkways were a bit eerie and we imagined could be quite claustrophobic to some. Eventually we were back into the fields bearing right to join a lane at Venn Farm which took us close to the main road. As we now had a town stretch looming, here was a good spot to have lunch.

Continuing, we joined the unpavemented main road to cross Black Bridge at the bottom of the hill over Castle Pill. We missed our turning just here and found our way into Milford Haven via a housing estate, and after directions from local residents, we took an overgrown footpath getting scratched and nettled in the process.

Back on the coast path proper, we carried on through the busy town of Milford Haven following the harbour and then finally climbed the hill out of the town through Hakin. We dropped down to the beach at Gelliswick to take a grassy track giving us some welcome relief from the last few miles of road walking.

At first the scenery was slightly marred by the tanks of the Amoco refinery, but soon we were low enough down the footpath to put the huge tanks out of sight, and round the next bend the world of oil was completely forgotten as we spotted Sandy Haven half a mile away.

Tankers on the jetty near Milford Haven

Jean and Norma came to meet us and we walked the last few hundred yards together to the car on the caravan park where we enjoyed relaxing with a snack and coffee.

Resting at Sandy Haven

Our new B&B was at Skerryback Farm on the north side of Sandy Haven. Finding our way into the farm was not without some difficulty, but once in we were made very welcome by Mr and Mrs Williams. The accommodation was good and we had an enjoyable dinner before going out for a drive round Dale to watch the sun set over the horizon—it was magic. We really don't want these breaks to end.

Then it was back to Skerryback and a good bed for our last night of the holiday.

Day 37 Musselwick to Newgale 15 miles

Before leaving Skerryback, Dave and I had a chat with Mr Williams who was a bit of a walker himself and had done parts of the Pembrokeshire Coast Path. He was very interested in our venture regards walking the entire Welsh coastline. He'd not heard of anyone doing likewise and wished us well to complete it. We're sure we will.

It was a short drive back to Marloes and we soon found the lane out to the Beacon where we had set off from on Saturday. Again we crossed the field to Black Rock and Musselwick Sands, this time turning right walking a very easy path on fairly low cliffs. The weather was brilliant again.

We reached the Nab Head passing a beautifully constructed stone wall which separated the path from Kensington Estate. The Barons of Kensington at one time owned the St. Brides Estate. Attractive parkland surrounds the Victorian 'castle' which was the baronial residence.

Eventually the trail descended to the pretty little cove of St. Bride's Haven. The most unusual feature of St. Bride's was the colour of the cliffs—almost bright red. It is a very popular spot for visitors. It offers a 'Victorianised' church, two walled gardens and a large and well-built lime kiln. There is a fairly large car park and grassy banks for picnics. In the cliffs near the lime kiln, coastal retreat has exposed the ends of stone-lined coffins in the old graveyard. After crossing the short beach, passing the boathouse, we were back on to the cliff footpath and although it was pretty exposed, it was still easy going.

Just before turning eastwards, we crossed Mill Haven and the inlets of Brandy Bay and Dutch Gin Bay, and then had a mile and a half stretch to Borough Head. As we made our steep descent from the headland, we ran into a plague of huge flying insects. There were millions of them flying seemingly blind into us and sticking to our clothes and skin. 'Black helicopters' we called them. This lasted for a good half a mile, and it was only on the lower slopes of the hill that we got rid of them, and although they didn't sting or bite, nevertheless this wasn't a pleasant section.

The path dropped through a lovely wooded area. Here we noticed many of the tree tops had been scorched and killed by the salt spray and strong wind blasts. This coast must certainly take a battering from the winter gales. Many trees and bushes were permanently bent away from the sea.

We joined a road for a couple of hundred yards before returning to a track over the cliffs, passing above the site of an abandoned sailing lifeboat station which operated between 1882 and 1922. We arrived at Little Haven. This is a pretty holiday village and sits in a deep narrow valley. At one time it was a coal port. Now it has inns, shops and a large car park, but road access is difficult via very steep hills on all sides.

Although we could have walked across the sands, we chose to stick with the narrow road through the village for half a mile to reach the busier Broad Haven where we stopped for lunch surrounded by jackdaws, although in all honesty, we didn't know they were jackdaws until we consulted Dave's 'Guide to British birds' book whilst we sat eating. For the uneducated, jackdaws are black with darkish grey heads—so there!

Little Haven

As we headed towards Black Point, warning signs of cliff erosion indicated an alternative path running parallel to the coast path just inside a hedge through farm fields. Just as the paths parted for a change, we met walkers coming from the opposite direction. Certainly, we've not seen many on our walks so far. The alternative path carried on for well over another mile and then joined a downhill road past Druidston Villa. A mile later brought us to Nolton Haven, another of Pembrokeshire's delightful creeks.

Now it was on to the final stretch of the day's walk. We passed the unusual rock formation of Rickett's Head, and just further on we saw traces of old colliery workings. Trefrane Cliff Colliery was worked from 1850 to 1905, with coal exported from Nolton Haven by sea. Newgale Sands came into view and it was not far to the car park and beach cafe where Jean and Norma were waiting. After a pot of tea, we were ready to head home.

This has been such a perfect break with everything going right.

We'd judged the tides at Dale and Sandy Haven, had glorious weather, good accommodation and brilliant scenery—what more could we wish for. We've walked well over 600 miles now, and when we get the pleasure we've had over the past few days, in a way, we don't want it to end.

CHAPTER SEVENTEEN

June 1995

Day 38 Nottage to Port Talbot 9 miles

Loughor to Llanelli 4 miles

For the first time, we managed to have a full week's holiday with an added bonus. Going back to Day 6 when we decided to have a weekly bet on the horses, thanks to two good wins of £211 and £319, we found we had accumulated around £800 in the 'kitty', so this break should cost us very little—can't be bad.

As we were now less than two hundred miles away from our goal, now was the time to plan the finishing point. We decided it would be somewhere on the Glamorgan Heritage Coast Path which runs from Aberthaw to Porthcawl, so calculating the the start point of this walking week was important. Lavernock Point, where we finished in south Wales last time, to Port Talbot, where we started the Gower peninsula, are roughly forty five miles apart, so assuming that we could walk thirty six miles in two days, this left nine miles to get out of the way on the journey to Pembrokeshire. Obviously, we had to calculate nine miles back from Port Talbot and walk from there. This turned out to be a place called Nottage, just outside Porthcawl.

The weather was fair as we arrived at the roundabout approaching Nottage where we left Norma and Jean who went off to explore Porthcawl. Once through the village just above the the promenade we had to pass through a field packed with tents belonging to 'Hell's Angels' who were having some sort of rally. They were a tough looking bunch and definitely not our scene, but in fairness many of them spoke as we passed.

For a while we were on a busy road, then a quieter lane led us through a pleasant section with the playing area of a golf course on either side of the road. Eventually we crossed the M4 motorway via a bridge and found a track through scrubland which ran parallel to the motorway. Then it was back onto road again, finally joining the main road. All this road walking had not been really enjoyable, and imagine our horror when we later found out we could have walked virtually all the way to Port Talbot on a beach. Looking at the map, we thought the private golf course prevented us from doing this, but it couldn't be helped.

The girls drove alongside just before reaching Port Talbot and after a short stop together, Dave and I walked the last half mile to Junction 40, our starting point of last time, thus completing another link in this walking chain. Then it was into the car for the drive to Loughor.

We had lunch in the car and, as we ate, noticed a few drops of rain. We calculated that we really needed to walk the four miles into Llanelli whatever the weather, otherwise we would find it difficult to fit in the whole unwalked section and we certainly didn't want to come all this way on a future occasion just to walk four miles. So we set off, having arranged to meet the girl at a particular road junction in Llanelli—what a mistake!

After only about a mile of walking, the rain began to get heavier and soon we were getting a soaking. Arriving at the outskirts of Llanelli town, we discovered to our horror that the intended meeting with Jean and Norma was impossible as the road we had suggested to meet, had been replaced by a new ring—road. Unable to contact them, we just had to hope that they would drive around trying to find us, and having walked into the town centre, we back-tracked down the way we had just done, simply to give them a better chance. Besides, the town was getting quite busy now, as people were finishing their Saturday shopping and it was nearly tea time. After about an hour of wandering around in the heavy downpour, in which Dave and I split up, with me standing in the middle of a roundabout, they found us—were we relieved! Well done girls.

Changing into dry clothes at the roadside didn't prove easy, but we managed and soon forgot all the discomforts of the afternoon as we headed off towards St. Petrox and our stay with Mrs Matthias at Bangeston Farm. Unfortunately, this time she no longer did an evening meal, so we found a Chinese restaurant in Pembroke town. We had tried a lovely little bistro called 'Malone's', only to find they were fully booked, but we were able to reserve a table for Monday evening. Then it was back to the farmhouse to get ready for tomorrow's stint.

Day 39 Manorbier to Freshwater West
20 miles

We woke to find it blowing very hard, not something you want on a clifftop path. We had planned originally to walk from Freshwater West, our last stopping point of the Pembrokeshire Coast Path, but on checking the wind direction, we felt reversing the walk was more prudent as we'd have the wind directly behind us. One good thing, it was lovely and sunny.

We set off from the firm sandy beach at Manorbier, having left the girls to visit Manorbier Castle. This splendid Norman castle dominates the northern side of the valley, while the modern settlement is a little inland. There is a pretty church with a tall Norman style tower. The 12th century writer, Gerald of Wales was born here in 1146. In his books, he described the area as 'the pleasantest spot in Wales'.

We were quickly into yet more glorious scenery and passed Swanlake Bay before reaching Freshwater East beach which we crossed via the the sand dunes, followed by the climb towards Trewent Point giving magnificent views in all directions. Just over two miles later, we were at Stackpole Quay and climbed the steps to take us back onto the coast path and on to the next bay—Barafundle. Swanlake, Stackpole and now Barafundle, all had a magical ring to their names, and all had magical scenery too, particularly Barafundle. This was so beautiful—secluded and totally unspoilt. It is accessible only via the coastal path. We had a short break perched above the sandy beach.

The stone steps down to the beach and the walled walkway on the north face of the bay were built by the Cawdor family of Stackpole, and still conjure up images of crinolined ladies flouncing their way down to the sands. We felt a sense of just wanting to stay there and take in the peace of the surroundings, but we had to press on.

Past Stackpole Head which we cut across without going out to the viewing point, we had more pleasures in store as we came to Broad Haven beach, another little gem. This Broad Haven is simply a stretch of sand and not to be confused with the village of Broad Haven which we walked last year. Beyond the dunes are the famous Bosherton Lily Ponds, another of Pembrokeshire's beauty spots. We had lunch among the rocks above the beach, enjoying the lovely sunshine whilst sheltering from the stiff breeze.

A small lagoon at Broad Haven near the outlet of the Bosherton Lily Ponds

After lunch we continued, now walking on permitted Ministry of Defence land. Fortunately, being Sunday, there was no firing in progress on the ranges, so we had an unrestricted path with no detours. This was very easy walking in open grassland interspersed with gorse bushes. The turf was lovely and springy as we belted along with the wind at our backs. We were really enjoying today's stretch.

Eventually we reached Stack Rocks where the clifftop section temporarily ended as Linney Head is out of bounds to the public. At Elegug Stacks we saw the famous Green Bridge of Wales, a natural arch sweeping across a void about eighty feet above the sea. There was an observation platform on the cliffs to view it, so naturally there were quite a few people about.

The Green Bridge of Wales

Turning away from the sea, we followed firstly a track, then a quiet road to take us into the village of Castlemartin, and from there it was just two and a half miles to the end of the day's walk.

As we neared Freshwater West, we passed a thatched seaweed-drying hut on a grassy bank above Little Furzenip—yet another magical name. This hut is the last in Pembrokeshire, rescued and preserved by the National Park Authority. The dried out red seaweed is commonly known as 'laver bread', much enjoyed by many Welsh.

Another hundred yards or so, and we were greeted by the magnificent sight of the sea at Freshwater West Bay, with huge waves being whipped into a mass of white spray by the strong wind. What a contrast this was from the last time we visited here arriving from the opposite direction, when there was hardly a ripple on the water. People were sitting out of the wind in their cars, Norma and Jean among them. They were so comfortable, that even after walking twenty miles, we were the ones who fetched the ice-creams from the van.

This had been a marvellous day's walking. We'd seen some of the prettiest bays of the whole Coast Path, and the sun and wind had certainly given us a good sun tan.

In the evening, we visited the same restaurant as last night, and enjoyed exchanging the events of the day with the girls, and as usual were planning tomorrows walk.

What a lovely day.

Day 40 Manorbier to Marros 19 miles

The strong wind of yesterday had dropped to a pleasant breeze and with still lots of sun, it was perfect walking weather for our last day in Pembrokeshire.

Leaving the farmhouse, we were soon at Manorbier again leaving the beach on a gently sloping path to the cliff top. At Presipe, an attractive sandy bay, we missed the path and ended up on Ministry of Defence property at Old Castle Head, but soon realised our mistake and scrambled back up to join the proper path. The army has cleared many old buildings, reclaimed some land and released the area between the headland and the housing estate on the main road, permitting a realignment of the Coast Path. We followed the fingerposts around the fenced perimeter and this led to an old army building now converted into a fine modern youth hostel.

We missed out intentionally the National Trust owned peninsula of Lydstep Point, and descended to Lydstep Haven, a longish beach, passing in front of the large caravan park along the promenade and leaving the beach at the far end, climbing to the clifftop quite steeply. Fortunately, as with Castlemartin, the firing range at Penally Camp was not in use and we had an uninterrupted easy walk to Giltar point before swinging round and down to Tenby South Beach. We walked the length of the beach and left by the steps to continue through the town centre.

Once through, we emerged on to the North Beach, and towards the far end by some ornamental gardens above the beach, we stopped for lunch.

Besides eating, lunch stops always mean a change of socks and shirts, plus an opportunity to carry out running repairs to the old feet. This is easily managed and accepted on cliff paths, but going through the routine on a popular promenade drew a few stares from passers-by at our steaming socks, plastered bare feet and the white trail of Johnson's talcum powder starting to blow into the flower beds.

We continued for a short while on the road and climbed the hill to take us clear of the town. Soon the coast path signs led us to the cliffs and an undulating section, particularly the very steep ascent through Lodge Valley, a lovely small pine forest. The smell of the pine was gorgeous. In fact, on this part of the coast, there were quite a few small woods and copses to pass through, and at times the sea was hidden from view. Then just after entering Rhode Wood, we took the diverted path to the sands which led us into Saundersfoot, although the racing incoming tide meant we had literally minutes to make it before being cut off. We just made it.

Once on Saundersfoot Beach we were able to cross on the firm sand above the Mean High Water line until leaving to pass through a tunnel which originally housed a narrow-gauge railway track which connected the local collieries to Saundersfoot harbour: There were two more tunnels all unlit and for a time we were in total darkness. Obviously being a popular holiday resort, there were quite a few people ambling around in these tunnels which meant very slow progress.

The low cliffs of this railway track stretch are notoriously unstable and we noticed many areas of loose ironstone rock were held onto the cliff face by strong netting. There is an alternative path which passes above the cliffs if there is any chance of danger, but today we didn't need to use it.

We descended on a road to Wiseman's Bridge, climbed the hill by the Inn and returned to the cliff top again. Then it was over the last stile of the 479 which have to be negotiated in the course of the National Trail.

Amroth, the finish of the Coast Path, was soon reached. It was a bit sad really, as we've had so much pleasure from over 180 miles of magnificent walks in some of the most picturesque scenery you can get. A plaque on the little bridge informs that the National Trail was officially opened on the 16th of May, 1970 by Wynnford Vaughan Thomas, although in fact it was 17 years in the planning stage.

We crossed the stream and we were now in Carmarthenshire.

There was a steep climb on the road out of Amroth which we stayed on for a couple of miles passing a wood on our right, heavy with the distinctive smell of wild garlic growing there. We had taken longer than we had intended today, and as we hadn't arranged a specific meeting place with the girls, other than we would be on this particular road heading towards Pendine Sands, we were relieved when they met up with us as we reached Marros.

In the evening we had a lovely meal at Malone's in Pembroke, even though it cost a bit more than we usually spend. Still we enjoyed it. Then it was back to Bangeston Farm to pack ready to move on.

Day 41 Marros to Llanstephan 20 miles

Yesterday, after leaving Bangeston Farm, we had a break from walking and decided to spend the day with the girls, showing them parts of the Coast Path we had covered over the last two days visiting Broad Haven, Stackpole Quay, Barafundle, Tenby and Saundersfoot. The four of us walked the Stackpole Quay to Barafundle cliff path and back, and they were as smitten as us. Then late afternoon we drove to Llangain, a small village near to Carmarthen to find our B&B accommodation at Glog Farm, the home of Maureen and Clive Gribble. Jean had booked this by telephone from Tenby, picked purely at random from our holiday guide, but what a choice it turned out to be.

We had a rather inauspicious start when Dave fell half way up the narrow stairs with his heavy suitcase, then couldn't get up for laughing. Mrs Gribble must have wondered what she had let herself in for, but we soon settled in to what was more super accommodation. The evening meal was brilliant with huge portions of real farmhouse cooking, and this morning's breakfast was more than substantial.

So to today's walk.

Clog Farm

We had quite a long drive from Llangain to Marros, but getting an early breakfast had helped and by 9.45am we had left the lay-by at Marros and were heading down the hill to Pendine Sands. The hard, firm, flat sand which stretches over six miles has been used in the past for land speed record attempts, among them Sir Malcolm Campbell in the 1920s, besides the many who have learnt to drive there.

Today unfortunately, the red warning flags were flying on the Ministry of Defence firing range, forcing us to take to the road after only a hundred yards or so.

The weather was pleasant for walking as we climbed the hill and made our way to Laugharne—pronounced Larne, where the poet Dylan Thomas spent most of his life living in the Boat House overlooking the peaceful estuary of the River Taf. We passed the church and cemetery where he is buried.

The road was quite busy and it wasn't a particularly exciting stretch, but soon we reached the outskirts of St. Clears. Before arriving at the village itself, we found a footpath which took us round to the Boat Club. As we were now off the main road, here was a good place to stop and have lunch.

While we sat eating, we could see on the other side of the river, the track we needed coming to a dead end at an electricity substation. Our actual path would or should have diverted from the track and follow farmland to join lanes leading to Llanstephan. This was not to be.

After lunch we made our way onto the track and although reaching the sub-station, there was no sign of a footpath, just an overgrown mass of brambles and nettles. Obviously, the farmer had not bothered to maintain the path as it would go across his land. So the half mile we had walked for nothing became a mile by the time we'd returned to the Boat Club bridge. We tried a path to the left and asked two farm labourers for directions. They pointed out a footpath by the farm but were none too specific, and eventually, despite trying to get through the farmyard and giving up, we decided to create a path ourselves round the back of a farmhouse to avoid an evil looking dog. Through a hedge and over a field, and we were in the lane we wanted. A short way down we did see a footpath sign, obviously the other end end of our original planned route. The path was totally overgrown and confirmed what we had found in north Wales, that many farmers aren't the most cooperative when it comes to maintaining footpaths.

This had turned out to be a real messy day, especially as we had just finished the Pembrokeshire Coast Path. There couldn't have been a greater contrast.

Although the rest of the walk was all in country lanes, it was quite pleasant as there was very little traffic about, and eventually we arrived at Llanstephan. This is a pleasant little village near the shore on the land between the estuaries of the Taf and the Tywi rivers, protected by a 12th century castle set between the village and the sea. We followed the road round past the castle and from there onto the water's edge at a grassy area called The Green where we hoped to have met the girls, but this time there was no sign of them, so we continued on the road to Llangain confident they would find us, and sure enough, a mile further on they turned up.

Back at Glog Farm we had an even larger meal than last night—not one, but two huge pork chops for the main course—scrumtious! All this and watching 'Coronation Street' at the same time, as Maureen had moved the television to a convenient position for us. It was just like being at home.

Day 42 Llanstephan to Kidwelly
20 miles

It was cooler but still sunny as we returned to the lay-by just outside Llanstephan and continued on the B4312 until about a mile off Llangain. There was a turning off here, a lane which climbed very steeply, but we didn't mind this as we prefer stiff hills to the busy traffic on the main roads.

Eventually, in Llangain village, we joined the main road again, and this time there was no escape and we had a few miles of road including the walk through the centre of Carmarthen town, leaving down a dual-carriageway, not what we'd call very coastal pathish.

We had made a conscious decision early into our venture that certain walks needn't be tackled. Yesterday's and today's walks have really only been following river estuaries. Strictly speaking, St. Clears and Carmarthen are not seaside towns and therefore not on a coastal route and we could and should have walked to Laugharne and driven round the two estuaries to resume at Ferryside, saving thirty two miles in the bargain, but as we've been enjoying ourselves so much, we decided that we'd walk them anyway.

A mile on the other side of Carmarthen, we joined a minor road which took us through the village of Croesyceilog. It was very quiet around here and made for quite pleasant walking. The lane continued until reaching the main Carmarthen to Llanelli road which we followed for a short distance before leaving down a track sign-posted 'Ferryside'. A few-hundred yards along, we stopped for lunch in a farm field.

The lanes for the next few miles were very narrow, often forcing us to back into the hedge whenever a car passed, but eventually we came to a pleasant road past woodlands and finally swung round at the bottom of the gradual descent into Ferryside village. Since starting our venture we have hardly stopped talking—often rubbish—and on this particular stretch we were discussing how many paces at a thirty inch stride we had taken in total. Mind blowing conversation this, but it all helps to pass the time.

Ferryside is a one-street village with a railway station, and through the level-crossing gates a walkway onto a small beach with Llanstephan directly opposite. What a pity some enterprising bod didn't run an actual ferry service from Llanstephan. With a name like Ferryside, presumably sometime in the past there had been a crossing. It would have saved us an awful lot of walking round the estuaries.

We left the road just outside the village and followed a lane coming very close to the river estuary. This was a much better walk now. For the last two miles we overlooked the mud flats leading to Cefn Sands with the Gower Peninsula in the far distance. We passed a quaint pond teeming with lots of ducks. We arrived at Kidwelly and made our way to the castle where our faithful back-up team were waiting having enjoyed a guided tour of the place.

In the evening after our meal, we had a drive out to the nearby pub, but it was a pretty uninspiring place. We didn't stay too long and were soon back to get ready for tomorrow. but not for walking—it was to be a day off spent with the girls.

Day 43 Llanelli to Kidwelly 9 miles

Yesterday we had our day out with Norma and Jean, actually driving the total route of our previous day's walk, including stopping off at the duckpond. If it had been left to Jean, we would have stayed all morning—she's an absolute sucker for ducks. We then spent the rest of the day at the Llanelli Wildlife Centre. This was a very enjoyable visit with yet more ducks. Jean was by now in 'seventh heaven'.

We ended the day with another super dinner and a Maureen special, strawberry and kiwi fruit pavlova.

Now we were into the last day of the holiday with just a morning walk to complete the unwalked stretch from last Saturday.

The weather wasn't too promising for today with a very poor forecast, but it didn't turn out to be too bad, and what rain we had lasted only minutes.

It was a fairly average walk once we had left Llanelli, very flat and all on pavement, but it's all part of the project and had to be done. We covered the nine and a bit miles in two and a half hours, that's averaging just under four miles an hour, not bad we thought.

We met up with the girls once more at Kidwelly Castle and decided to have lunch in the small restaurant by the castle before leaving for home. It was a lovely journey back through Builth Wells and Knighton where we stopped to get some information on Offa's Dyke for a possible future project.

We looked back on what had been a wonderful week's holiday. First of all, the bookie had provided for nearly all our expenses so that Dave and I had to put just £15 each to the 'kitty', and secondly we had walked all we had intended, about 102 miles with no gaps left. Finally the 'icing on the cake' was Glog Farm. The only downside was saying goodbye to the Pembrokeshire Coast Path.

The end was now in sight—only sixty odd miles to go.

CHAPTER EIGHTEEN

1996

Day 44 Menai Bridge 0.5 mile

Barmouth Bridge 1 mile

Aberdovey to Machynlleth 10 miles

Tre'rddol to Ynyslas 4 miles

The time had arrived to plan the finish of our venture. We reviewed the situation to see that we hadn't walked the Menai Bridge, Barmouth to Fairbourne via the toll bridge, the Dovey estuary and the south Wales stretch between Nottage and Lavernock Point. This could all be covered in just three day's walking, so we had mixed emotions as we set off from Stoke—sad that it would be all over, but satisfied that we had, hopefully achieved our goal. So it was back to Anglesey where it had all started.

We left early in the morning in lovely weather, and having crossed the Britannia Bridge, drove to the Menai Bridge, our first port of call. It was hard to believe that having made all these trips to Anglesey, we hadn't actually walked the Bridge. Ten minutes was all it took. Then it was into the car for the drive to Barmouth about twenty miles away. We were in Barmouth for 7.30, even before there was anyone there to collect the 30p toll charge, and walked the mile stretch over the bridge while the girls took the car round the Mawddach estuary.

We met up on the approach to Fairbourne. and then it was the next leg of the journey driving down to Aberdovey arriving by about 9am. As said earlier, the Dovey estuary really is a pain in the backside. The main problem is the fact that the walk, particular the Aberystwyth side of the estuary, is on a busy road with no footpath for most of the way—highly dangerous to say the least. We agreed to walk as far as Machynlleth, meet Norma and Jean at the railway station, and then decide on whether to try down the far side or not.

The walk from Aberdovey on the main road was very easy going but nothing spectacular. It annoyed us that we were walking alongside the railway line that would have got us round the estuary but we just couldn't use it—very frustrating.

At the village of Pennal, the local Church was having it's fund raising day, and, as we passed, the ladies manning the 'plants' stall outside invited us in and wouldn't take no for an answer. We spent £1 each on a cup of coffee and a piece of chocolate cake and had a chat with the only man present. We told him of our problem crossing the Dovey, but he only confirmed what others had said—it couldn't be done without trespassing on the railway.

We were in Machynlleth by lunchtime and the girls were waiting. On the way from Aberdovey, looking across the estuary we could see how traffic was building up, and after lunch in the car, we made the decision, in the interests of safety, to forget the next nine miles drive down to the junction of the B4353, Tre'r-ddol, and walk to Ynyslas.

On arriving at Ynyslas, we had a drink and half an hour's rest before setting off for the long drive to Barry in south Wales where our next B&B accommodation had been booked. It had been a right hectic day.

It was after 7pm when we arrived at New Farm. We let ourselves in with the key left under a flowerpot, pre-arranged by Mrs Hardy as she and Mr Hardy were going to a wedding that day. Considering we had never met them, they were very trusting.

Unfortunately being so late, by the time we had changed etc, we had difficulty finding somewhere to eat. We tried one place, the 'Six Bells Inn' at Penmark thinking we could get a bar type meal. The owner, Don, a jolly dapper little gent with cravat and blazer welcomed us and said really they only did restaurant meals and we needed to have booked as the food was out of this world, prepared by his Michelin-starred chef. We booked dinner for Monday evening to celebrate. hopefully, the end of 'the Walk'. For this evening however, we eventually got fixed up at the local Toby Inn. The food was very good and we decided to reserve a table for tomorrow evening when they had a bargain price meal.

What a busy day—a very early start, four walks and miles of road travel. Little wonder we all slept soundly.

Day 45 Lavernock to Nash Point
21 miles

The finishing point of the whole walk had now been decided. It would end at Nash Point on the Glamorgan Heritage Coast Path.

But, oh dear. For our penultimate walk we woke to the sound of rain, and this was still continuing as we left the farm for the drive to Lavernock Church and, although not heavy, it was not too pleasant.

The lane from Lavernock took us on to the main Cardiff to Barry road which we followed through Sully and then into Barry town. Barry isn't a particularly attractive place and we weren't sorry when we finally left by following the road to Porthkerry Country Park. This was far more pleasant and the trail in the park eventually led down to a small beach and after a short cliff path section we passed through the caravan park. The rain had eased a little as we made our way across the railway line where we were on hand to help a British Rail chap lift a gate crossing the line back onto it's hinges.

Having done our good deed for the day, we next passed through the village of Rhoose just as the rain returned. It was getting close to lunchtime now but finding a place to stop was difficult as there were hedges on both sides of the road, so when we came to a lay-by, we parked ourselves on the kerb to eat—very uncomfortable and made worse by the constant drizzle. Imagine our frustration when, after resuming, just round the next bend, there was a picnic bench on the grass verge.

The next stretch took us on to a busy main road, but after about three quarters of a mile we saw the sign to lead us to the Glamorgan Heritage Coast Path which we eventually reached on the far side of West Aberthaw Dower station at Gileston

The Glamorgan Heritage walk is a protected coastline which stretches for 18 miles between Aberthaw in the east to Porthcawl in the west, a lovely shoreline with superb sea views and has a rich wildlife. In 1972, it was the first coastline in Wales to attract 'Heritage Coast' status.

It was much better weather now, breezy and coolish, but at least the sun appeared and we had some blue sky. After a morning of walking on concrete in the pouring rain, we were back on the clifftop. This was more like it.

The first part of the Heritage Way was less than very ordinary.

For a few hundred yards we walked over scrubland, and the view of the sea was obstructed by a row of huge concrete blocks, presumably some form of breakwater, but soon we were on a decent path which climbed to the clifftop. We were to remain on this track for the rest of the day and there were excellent views all round. It was just like the Pembrokeshire coast all over again.

Once we had reached the top the track was very easy going, and we actually met some families out walking, although many were hardly equipped for the muddy conditions. At one point we crossed a walled stile with a plaque commemorating a visit by King George V. We didn't realise he did coastal path walking in his spare time.

At last we reached Nash Point, quite a popular place. There are twin lighthouses which arrange tours for visitors, and also a nature reserve. Just past the footpath from the lighthouse, there was a kiosk selling snacks and drinks. It was doing good business and, as we were in advance of Jean and Norma, we bought a good warming mug of tea—enjoyable and very welcome after today's exertions in the wet.

The girls eventually turned up and we spent half an hour together just relaxing. As we sat we were looking for something that would act as our finishing line, something that we could touch together. We spotted the Nature Reserve signpost—that would be it.

The evening meal was back at the Toby Inn again—very good value. Then it was a return to the farm to prepare for the final day.

Weatherwise it looked as if tomorrow would be good which is just what we'd hoped for. It would have been disappointing to have ended on a wet note, so let's hope the weathermen are right.

Day 46 Nottage to Nash Point 16 miles

After breakfast we drove, for the last time, to our start point at Nottage roundabout in perfect walking weather—the forecast was right. There was just a little hint of sadness as we put on the walking gear, that today would be the end of our Welsh coastline venture. We said cheerio to the girls and set off on the last leg.

Arriving in Porthcawl we made our way to the promenade and dropped to the sands for a short stretch before returning to a walkway leading to the Coney Beach Pleasure Park which was getting quite busy even for so early in the day. Passing a large caravan park, we reached, Newton and the start of the western end of the Heritage Path.

The path was quite easy to follow at first but gradually, as we got deeper into the dunes, other paths were springing up out of nowhere and the route became more difficult to follow. Soon we realised we were heading towards the sea and the inlet at Ogmore.

This would have been alright if the walk had only been to there, but we needed to be across the other side of the inlet, and as the crossing point was at Ogmore Castle at the head of the inlet, we had to head away from the sea and take to the high dunes of Newton Burrows.

Eventually the track became clearer and soon we were overlooking Ogmore Castle. We made our way down a huge expanse of sand and followed a lane past the beautiful church at Merthyr-Mawr. The lane turned into a track which crossed the river by the castle and soon we were on the busier road leading to Ogmore-on-Sea. Guessing that the beach area would be crowded in the nice weather we decided to find a secluded spot just off the road to have lunch.

Resuming, we made our way towards Ogmore, now walking on a grassy path running parallel to the road—much easier on the old feet. As we had predicted, it was busy at Ogmore. We threaded our way through the holidaymakers and by chance came across Jean and Norma sitting relaxing after lunching in the car. There was just time to have a few minutes chat before we were on our way again, continuing on a decent path running along the cliff top.

About four miles along the path, we reached Southerndown, a very popular area with lots of people about. We climbed the hill on the far side of the beach and had our final stop for a snack. Ten minutes later and we were on the way again and into the last five miles.

The Path left the cliff top shortly after and headed across two fields to join a road. We followed this for a short way and then, just before reaching Monknash, a signpost led us back through fields and towards the sea. Although we were less than a mile from Nash Point, we couldn't see the lighthouse. There were quite a few People walking down to the small beach and we tagged along behind. Then just before reaching the cove, the path bore left up the hill and as we reached the top, there it was,Nash Point Lighthouse.

The path dropped into a valley and now we were just two hundred yards away from our goal. There were no brass bands, television or press to welcome us, just our faithful back-up team who came down the path to greet us and walk the last hundred yards with us. Dave and I placed our hands simultaneously on the Nature Reserve signpost at 4.40pm, Monday 27th May 1996. We'd done it.

Done it

There was no champagne to celebrate with, just our usual 'cuppa' as we sat down to relax for half an hour.

After our well earned rest, we headed off back to prepare for our evening out at the 'Six Bells' at Penmark, and what an experience that was. We had a very high class meal with very high prices to match £130 for the four of us, but it did include champagne to toast the completion of our venture.

Next morning we went into Cardiff for a relaxing stroll around, seeing the proposed regeneration of the docks area. This will be a great place to visit in the future. Then we moved up to Caerphilly where we stopped for lunch at 'The Green Man'—£3.95 for steak and chips—a bit different from last night's 'gourmet feast' but still very enjoyable.

On the way home, we reflected not only on this little break, but relived some of the moments of the whole walk. However, there was one thing we kept coming back to and it was niggling us. We had walked the coastline of Wales EXCEPT FOR NINE MILES. We couldn't let that beat us.

And so . . . .

CHAPTER NINETEEN

November 1996

Day 47 Tre'r-ddol to Machynlleth
9 miles

On 23rd November, the opportunity arose to walk the missing nine miles of the Walk.

The weather leading up to the Saturday had been diabolical all week with snow all over the country. Even as we travelled down to Wales early on the Saturday morning, we ran into a blizzard, but the forecast for later was not too bad for the area with some sunny spells promised. In fact, the weather in some way helped because it would deter people travelling unnecessarily and thereby lessening the chance of the winding road we had to walk, being too busy.

We started from Tre'r-ddol leaving Norma and Jean to drive to Borth to find somewhere selling hot drinks. The weather wasn't too bad and although we had set off in jackets, we were soon down to a sweater. The road was all flat and very easy going, just as it had been on the Aberdovey side of the estuary. We could see Aberdovey and Pennal quite clearly on a lovely crisp morning, and the good pace we set kept us nice and warm.

The road passed through Furnace and Eglwys Fach where, just after there was a turning into the hills we could have taken to avoid the winding road, but we were quite happy to stay as we were, pleased that the road was much quieter than we had hoped for. Mind you, we wouldn't have fancied this in high season traffic, and we felt the decision back in May to miss out this stretch, was quite justifiable.

At one point just before Derwenlas, the road came very close to the railway line. We climbed over the gate and sat on the rails to have a short break. When we stopped we realised just how cold it was, and we were ready to get going again as soon as possible.

The last mile was now on a proper footpath and soon we, arrived in Machynlleth. We made our way through the Saturday shoppers and also a large gathering of people. Surely folk hadn't heard of our venture and turned out to greet us. No, they were just there for a wedding.

As we climbed the slope of the approach to the railway station and the waiting girls, we didn't have quite the same feeling as we had at Nash Point, but it was the outcome which was the important thing. We could now say, without any shadow of doubt, that we had walked the entire coastline of Wales, all 792 miles of it. Mission accomplished.

EPILOGUE

So ended our walk round the coastline of Wales.

From the pipe-dream we had those years ago, now at last we had achieved our goal.

We have spent forty seven days walking 792 miles, often venturing into places we had never heard of let alone visited, many just names on a map.

We have had the pleasure of seeing so much of the countryside as we have travelled to the coast.

Accommodation has ranged from bungalows, hotels, guest houses, farmhouses and even a lighthouse.

Evening meals have been eaten in pubs, Chinese restaurants, fish and chip shops, bistros and posh restaurants, besides the dinners we've had at our half-board accommodation,

Walks have varied from the hard concrete road stretches laden with traffic, to peaceful cliff paths and secluded beaches.

We've walked in blistering sun and torrential rain.

Norma and Jean have visited castles, markets, craft shops, slate mines, silver mines, butterfly farms, bird sanctuaries, aquariums museums, stately homes and garden centres as well as going on a conducted nature ramble.

All in all, it has been one tremendously enjoyable experience for the four of us.

The idea of doing such a walk would probably never have blossomed at all had it not been for our dogs, Dave's black labrador, Gemma, and my red setter, Max. They're the ones who would regularly get us off our backsides to trudge endless miles round the lanes and fields of Loughborough and Stoke giving us a feel for walking. Sadly, neither of them were with us by the time we completed the venture, but they were often a topic of conversation as we journeyed on.

We have to admit, we couldn't have taken on this walk without the help of Jean And Norma, and we were grateful for the support they gave us—preparing the food, finding accommodation and above all being there to meet us at the end of a day's effort and sharing our experiences. They've certainly enjoyed it themselves despite often having to be up at 3.00am, although in fact, none of us ever found this a hardship—we considered this as part of the whole thing.

Planning the individual walks and meeting places was also part of the enjoyment, and there was always the thrill of setting off early in the morning wondering what each walk would have in store.

We hope that by setting down this account of our walk, perhaps it will encourage future generations of our families to try something similar. It isn't as difficult as you think, after all if we could do it, anyone can. We can promise one thing for sure, it will provide a most rewarding way to enjoy some of the natural beauty of our planet, and keep you fit as well.

We have so many lovely memories of our time in Wales, and we are unlikely ever, to forget such sights as the magnificence of the wild sea at Freshwater West, the glorious gorse and heather paths of Penbwchdy, the peaceful harbour at Solva, the bird and plant life on the clifftops, the beauty of secluded beaches at Broad Haven, Barafundle Bay and so many more.

In the future we hope to walk other paths. Offa's Dyke and the South West coast are already in the pipeline, but these are well prepared and established ways which have been walked by thousands. The 792 miles we have described was our walk.

Perhaps one day, we'll do it again.